THE ATTRIBUTES OF GOD

*Understanding Who the God
of the Bible Truly Is*

Ram Krishnamurthy

The Attributes of God

Understanding Who the God of the Bible Truly Is

by

Ram Krishnamurthy

This work may be freely copied and used without the author's permission.

ISBN: 9798870243245

Independently Published

First Edition

Unless otherwise indicated, Scripture quotations are taken from The Holy Bible, New International Version® NIV® Copyright © 1973, 1978, 1984, 2011 by Biblica, Inc. Used with permission. All rights reserved worldwide.

Scripture quotations marked (NASB®) are taken from the New American Standard Bible®, Copyright © 1960, 1971, 1977, 1995 by The Lockman Foundation. Used by permission. All rights reserved.

Scripture quotations marked (ESV) are taken from The Holy Bible, English Standard Version®, © 2001 by Crossway, a publishing ministry of Good News Publishers. Used by permission. All rights reserved.

Scripture quotations marked (NLT) are taken from the *Holy Bible*, New Living Translation, copyright ©1996, 2004, 2015 by Tyndale House Foundation. Used by permission of Tyndale House Publishers, Carol Stream, Illinois 60188. All rights reserved.

To

God, the blessed and only Ruler, the King of kings and Lord of lords, who alone is immortal and who lives in unapproachable light, whom no one has seen or can see. To him be honor and might forever. Amen.

—1 Timothy 6:15b-16

Contents

Preface: Using This Book 1
Introduction: Why Study the Attributes of God 5
Attribute 1: The Holiness of God 13
Attribute 2: The Power of God 23
Attribute 3: The Presence of God 39
Attribute 4: The Knowledge of God 51
Attribute 5: The Fatherhood of God 65
Attribute 6: The Love of God 75
Attribute 7: The Wisdom of God 89
Attribute 8: The Wrath of God 103
Attribute 9: The Faithfulness of God 115
Attribute 10: The Sovereignty of God 127
Attribute 11: The Patience of God 141
Attribute 12: The Unchanging Nature of God 153
Conclusion: Thank You 171
Acknowledgments 175
About the Author 178
Bibliography 180

PREFACE

Using This Book

Thank you so much for considering reading this book that covers twelve attributes of God. The goal is to aid the reader in gaining a good grasp of the true nature of the God of the Bible. While this is not an in-depth study of this vast subject and is not primarily written for scholars, it is still based on the solid foundation of the Scriptures.

Each chapter is generally short, containing applications for believers and appealing to non-Christians. Discussion questions are provided at the end of each chapter to prompt practical life changes. A Scripture verse is listed under each attribute for meditation and memorization. A list of hymns/songs is also added that can be used to praise God for a given attribute. And to complete each chapter, a short prayer is offered to help live in the light of that attribute.

Here are a few ways this book could be used:

- Private reading.

- Small group Bible study.

- Tool for discipling new believers. (It would be a helpful way to start new believers on the path to knowing and enjoying the glorious God of the Bible!)

- Given to a friend or family member who is not yet a Christian but may be open to knowing more about the God of the Bible.

- Pastors who may wish to teach their congregation about various attributes of God. (Song options are given at the end of each chapter to assist those who lead the music ministry when that specific attribute of God is preached.)

- In addition to the above, if you or someone you know struggles in some area of life, then even parts of this book can be helpful.

- For example, when struggling with anxiety, the chapter "The Presence of God" can be helpful.

- When things seem against you, the chapter "The Sovereignty of God" can calm the struggling soul.

- If there's a struggle to overcome sin, the chapters "The Holiness of God" and "The Love of God" can assist.

- If wrestling with a decision, the chapter "The Wisdom of God" can be of some guidance.

So, as you can see, this book can be used for various purposes. A list of resources is also given at the end were consulted while preparing this book, but they could also aid you toward a deeper understanding of this vital subject.

I sincerely pray that the Lord will be pleased to use this book to help you grow in your knowledge of Him and your love for Him.

By the way, no part of this book is copyrighted. Author credit is not needed either. So, please feel free to use it as required.

To God be all glory!

In Christ,

Ram Krishnamurthy

INTRODUCTION

Why Study the Attributes of God

A.W. Tozer, in his famous book, *The Knowledge of the Holy*, rightly said:

> *A right conception of God is basic not only to systematic theology but to practical Christian living as well...I believe there is scarcely an error in doctrine or a failure in applying Christian ethics that cannot be traced finally to imperfect and ignoble thoughts about God.*[1]

So, if we desire to live the Christian life in a pleasing and acceptable manner to God, we must strive to have a proper conception of Him. And since the God of the Bible can only be understood by His attributes, it's vital that we study them. So, that's the goal of this short book: to study and, as a result, grow in our understanding of God's attributes.

---

[1] Quoted in Grace Community Church, *Fundamentals of the Faith*, (Chicago, IL: Moody Publishers, 2009), p. 26.

I hope you will be encouraged and challenged to pursue a deeper study of this subject. It's a lifelong study that results in immense blessings—five of which are given below.

Five Blessings of Studying the Attributes of God

Blessing #1: It helps us to offer acceptable worship.

The writer of the book of Hebrews commands us to "worship God *acceptably* with reverence and awe" (Hebrews 12:28, italics mine). How can we do this unless we understand who He is? And since God can be understood only by His attributes, we must grow in our understanding of them to worship Him in a way that He deems acceptable.

Blessing #2: It pleases God.

Colossians 1:10 describes that a life honoring and pleasing to the Lord is one that's continually "growing in the knowledge of God." Since God is knowable only through His attributes, we can grow in the knowledge of God *only* if we study His attributes as revealed to us in the Bible. And that's what makes theology, which means the study of God, essential for Christian growth. It's a misunderstanding to think theology is only for the scholarly branch of Christianity. On the contrary, theology is for every Christian. Why? Because every Christian should seek to please God by growing in their understanding of His nature!

Blessing #3: It guards us against having a wrong view of God.

It's been said that a man's own character will necessarily be determined by the character of the god he worships. If our view of the God of the Bible is faulty, it will affect not only our worship of Him but also our character. That's why it's crucial to heed Tozer's warning at the beginning of this chapter. A lack of proper understanding of God's attributes will lead to a wrong view of God and result in a life that fails to please Him. That's why it's of great importance to study the attributes of God. Agreed, even a lifetime study of God's attributes will not yield a complete understanding of His attributes because it is impossible for finite creatures to understand an infinite God fully.

However, we are created in the image of God. That means we have the innate capacity to correlate certain truths about God. And having been re-created in Christ (2 Corinthians 5:17) and with the ongoing illuminating work of the indwelling Holy Spirit (1 Corinthians 2:13), we *can* know God more and more. Even after 25 years of ministry, Paul's persistent desire or goal was this: "I want to know Christ" (Philippians 3:10). May that be our continual goal as well.

Blessing #4: It produces joy in our hearts.

The Westminster Catechism states the chief end of man is to glorify God and enjoy Him forever. As we grow in our knowledge of God, our love for Him increases, and so does our obedience. As a result, the Holy Spirit produces more joy in our lives (Galatians 5:22). How encouraging are the words of the renowned preacher of the past, Charles Spurgeon:

> *Plunge yourself in the Godhead's deepest sea; be lost in His immensity; and you shall come forth as from a couch of rest refreshed and invigorated. I know nothing which can so comfort the soul; so calm the swelling billows of sorrow and grief; so speak peace to the winds of trial, as a devout musing upon the subject of the Godhead.*[2]

Blessing #5: It helps us to respond to suffering in a biblical manner.

Suffering is a reality in a broken world (Romans 8:20). Even Christians are not immune from it. And often, there are no perfect or even acceptable answers to the suffering we may face. During such times, we will be tempted to question God's ways, fall into great discouragement and despair, and even become distant from Him. However, as we grow in our understanding of His nature, our trust in Him increases. And as that happens, instead of seeking answers to the "why" aspect of suffering, we will find rest in God, knowing that He has not abandoned us and will bring us safely home as He promised (Philippians 1:6).

---

[2] Sermon titled "The Immutability of God, preached on January 7, 1855, as cited in *Fundamentals of the Faith*, p. 25.

Introduction: Why Study the Attributes of God

The godly man Job found this to be true. He faced unimaginable suffering and was struggling with many questions and wished he could present those questions directly to God (Job 13:3). But when God finally revealed Himself to Job, Job not only put his hands on his mouth but he also repented of speaking things he didn't understand (Job 40:4, 42:4-6). And even though Job never got answers to his questions, he could rest in simply growing in his understanding of God. The same is true for you and me. The more we understand God's character, the more we will handle suffering in a biblical manner, which is to continue clinging to Him by faith, not question His ways, not fall into discouragement and despair, and not distancing ourselves from Him.

I hope these five blessings motivate us to pursue a lifelong study of God's attributes. But before we study His attributes, let's look at a few basic truths about this subject.

BASIC TRUTHS CONCERNING THE ATTRIBUTES OF GOD

What it is. An attribute is a quality or characteristic that is inherent in a person. When referring to God's attributes, we are talking about the various qualities that are inherent and permanent in His nature and are revealed to us in the Scriptures.

What it is not. The various attributes of God are not component parts of God. In other words, God is not

10% love, 15% holy, 5% mercy, and so on. Each attribute describes His total being. For example, love is not a part of God's nature; God, in His whole being, *is* love. Holiness is not part of God's nature; God *is* holy in His entire being. Righteousness is not part of God's nature; God *is* righteous in His total being.

And neither can God compromise one of His attributes while exhibiting another. In other words, the same God who is love (1 John 4:8) is also the same God who exhibits wrath (Psalm 5:5). So, it is important not to conclude that because "God is love," He will eventually save all people. He who is love is also holy and exhibits wrath. That's why the statement, "God loves the sinner but hates the sin," should be stated with great caution.

While God does rescue repentant sinners because of His loving nature, He must and will eventually judge unrepentant sinners by casting them into everlasting hell because of His holy character. God does not just punish sin. He also punishes the sinner who continues in sin without turning to Him through faith in His Son, Jesus Christ. That's why when we study the attributes of God, we must be careful not to emphasize one attribute of His at the expense of the others. God is the sum of all perfections.

God's attributes can be broadly classified into 2 categories: incommunicable and communicable.

Incommunicable Attributes. These are attributes that belong to God exclusively. They are not passed down to us. Examples would be God's self-existence, omnipotence, omniscience, omnipresence, and so forth.

Communicable Attributes. These are attributes of God that we can possess to a limited extent. Examples would be love, mercy, kindness, and so on.

I admit that it is not always easy to classify some attributes as strictly belonging to one category and not to the other. For example, while omniscience is an incommunicable attribute, we humans possess knowledge, even though it is limited compared to the all-knowing God. So, we must be careful not to focus so much on the attribute category. Instead, the focus should be on the study of the attributes themselves.

With those preliminary thoughts, let's prayerfully study a few of God's attributes in the following pages.

ATTRIBUTE 1

The Holiness of God

The holiness of God refers not only to His complete separation from sin in all its forms but also to the fact that He is entirely pure and set apart from the rest of His creation.

Perhaps this analogy might help us better understand the above description of God's holiness:

> *What does it mean to be healthy? It's [not only] the absence of illness, but also a positive infusion of energy. Holiness is the absence of evil and the presence of positive right. In God, His holiness is a purity of being and nature as well as of will and act.*[3]

According to writer Paul Enns:

> *Many see holiness [of God] as the foremost attribute of all because holiness pervades all the*

---

[3] Charles Ryrie, *Basic Theology*, (Grand Rapids: MI, Zondervan, 1999) p. 42.

> *other attributes of God and is consistent with all He is and does. Several features are embraced in the holiness of God.*
>
> *It has a transcendent emphasis, indicating "He is absolutely distinct from all His creatures and is exalted above them in infinite majesty…Isaiah 57:15 describes His transcendence: He is "high and exalted," living on a "high and holy place."*
>
> *It has an ethical emphasis, indicating "He is separate from moral evil or sin." 'Holiness' points to God's majestic purity, or ethical majesty. The foundation of this emphasis is Leviticus 11:44,45: "Be holy, for I am holy." Because God is morally pure, He cannot condone evil or have any relationship to it (Psalm 11:4-6). In His holiness God is the moral and ethical standard; He is the law. He sets the standard.*[4]

Only once in Scripture is an attribute of God mentioned three times in succession: His holiness. Holiness, "as none other, is solemnly celebrated before the Throne of Heaven, the seraphim crying, 'Holy, holy, holy, is the Lord of hosts' (Isaiah 6:3)."[5] Indeed, holiness may well be the "attribute of all attributes."[6]

---

[4] Paul Enns, *The Moody Handbook of Theology*, (Chicago: IL, Moody, 2014) p. 199.
[5] Pink, Arthur W, *The Attributes of God*, (Grand Rapids: MI, Baker, 1975), p. 52.
[6] Ibid.

We can see God's holiness evidenced in at least three areas.

1. God's Holiness Is Evidenced by His Nature

God's holiness means He is completely separated from sin. This truth is evident from 1 John 1:5, where we are told, "God is light." Notice the text does not say God is a light among many other lights or that God has light. Instead, it says God *is* light. Just like "God is spirit" (John 4:24a) and "God is love" (1 John 4:8b), God is also holy in His essence. Here are some verses that highlight this theme:

> **Exodus 15:11** – *Who among the gods is like you, Lord? Who is like you—majestic in holiness, awesome in glory, working wonders?*

> **1 Samuel 2:2** – *There is no one holy like the Lord; there is no one besides you; there is no Rock like our God.*

2. God's Holiness Is Evidenced by His Works

God's holiness is seen not only in His nature but also in all creation and through the Scriptures.

In Creation. Genesis 1:31 clearly states that when God originally created everything, it was pure and without sin.

In the Scriptures. Romans 7:12 says, "So then, the law is holy, and the commandment is holy, righteous and good." That's why the Bible is called "The Holy Bible."

So, both in creation, also known as God's general revelation, which is limited in nature, and the Scriptures, also known as God's special revelation, where He reveals more of Himself, God's holiness is evidenced by His works. Stephen Charnock wrote, "Power is God's hand, omniscience His eye, mercy His bowels, eternity His duration, but holiness is His beauty."[7] No wonder those set free from sin's power see God's holiness as the most beautiful of all His attributes.

3. God's Holiness Is Evidenced by His Response to Sin

The apostle John *reinforces* the positive statement of truth that "God is light" (1 John 1:5a) by this statement: "In him there is no darkness at all" (1 John 1:5b). Since God is light, He cannot be the opposite of light, which is darkness. And just as light cannot be contaminated, God cannot have darkness in Him. That is why God hates all forms of sin because darkness refers to sin (John 3:19).

We read God's reaction to sin in Habakkuk 1:13, "Your eyes are too pure to look on evil; you cannot tolerate wrongdoing." Just as God perfectly loves what is pure, He also perfectly hates what is impure or unholy. Proverbs 15:9 states, "The LORD detests the way of the

---

[7] Quoted in A.W. Pink, *Attributes of God*, p. 52.

wicked, but he loves those who pursue righteousness." And because God hates what is evil, He must also punish that which is evil. The flood during Noah's time, the destruction of Sodom and Gomorrah, and Pharaoh and the Egyptians being judged for enslaving the Jews are a few examples to prove this fact.

But the supreme example of God's hatred for sin is seen in His judgment of His Son Jesus, who bore our sins on the cross. When the Lord Jesus bore our sins on the cross, God unleashed His full fury on His dearly loved Son. God did not reduce His holiness because His Son suffered on the cross. He did not lower His standard of righteousness to meet His Son's needs. That is how much God hates sin. He never makes any compromise with darkness.

Our Response to God's Holiness

So, what must be our response to God's holiness? The Apostle Peter captures it quite well in 1 Peter 1:14-16 (drawn from Leviticus 11:44-45 and 19:2), which states, "As obedient children, do not conform to the evil desires you had when you lived in ignorance. But just as he who called you is holy, so be holy in all you do; for it is written: 'Be holy, because I am holy.'" Once again, to quote Stephen Charnock, "This is the prime way of honoring God. We do not so glorify God by elevated admirations, or eloquent expressions or pompous services of Him, as when we aspire to a conversing with

Him with unstained spirits, and live *to* Him in living *like* Him."[8]

In our Lord's teaching concerning how we should pray, the first part of the petition begins with: "Hallowed be your name" (Matthew 6:9) or "May your name be kept holy" (NLT). And the best way to honor a holy God is by living a holy life ourselves. Imitation is the proper response to admiration! This old Puritan's prayer well captures the essence of a believer's longing to be holy since God is holy:

> *My God,*
>
> *I feel it is heaven to please thee, and to be what thou wouldst have me be. O that I were holy, as thou art holy, pure as Christ is pure, perfect as they Spirit is perfect!*
>
> *These, I feel, are the best commands in thy Book, and shall I break them? must I break them? am I under such a necessity as long as I live here?*
>
> *Woe, woe is me that I am a sinner, that I grieve this blessed God, who is infinite in goodness and grace...*
>
> *What shall I do to glorify and worship this best of beings? O that I would consecrate my soul and body to his service, without restraint, for ever!*
>
> *O that I could give myself up to him, so as never more to attempt to be my own! or have any will*

---

[8] Ibid

or affections that are not perfectly conformed to his will and his love!9

Hebrews 12:14b clearly states that "without holiness, no one will see the Lord." God's purpose in disciplining His children is that they might "share in his holiness" (Hebrews 12:10b). We are commanded to separate ourselves from everything that "contaminates both body and spirit, perfecting holiness out of reverence for God" (2 Corinthians 7:1b). We must continually present ourselves "as a living sacrifice, holy and pleasing to God" (Romans 12:1b). Don't these verses call for a radical dealing with sin and relentless pursuit for holiness fueled by His grace and reliance on the Holy Spirit?

That's why the starting point for those who have never placed their faith in Jesus is to turn to Him without delay. You cannot escape this holy God. The Bible clearly states that there is a future judgment coming. And if you die without having your sins forgiven through Jesus, your future is very dark indeed. The final place of residence for all such people will be the lake of fire (Revelation 20:14), also called hell (Matthew 5:29), where they will spend eternity in conscious pain and torment. Hell is also where Satan and his demons will be thrown for eternal punishment (Revelation 20:10; Matthew 25:41).

---

[9] Arthur Bennet, *The Valley of Vision* (Edinburgh: The Banner of Truth Trust, 2002), pp. 232-233.

So, I genuinely appeal to you in love: Turn from your sins and turn to Christ today. "Today, if you hear his voice, do not harden your hearts" (Hebrews 4:7b). Jesus is the only way by which your sins can be forgiven. It's through Jesus alone you can be reconciled with this holy God. Call out to Jesus to save you and, in that way, experience the joy of having your sins wiped clean. And then (and only then) you will have the power to pursue a holy lifestyle through the Holy Spirit—both in thought and action.

Remember, "God is light; in him there is no darkness at all" (1 John 1:5). God has nothing to do with darkness, and as His children, neither can we have anything to do with darkness. God's ways are always the best because it is the way of holiness. It is the way of life and light; there is no cause for stumbling or wandering. The higher our view of God, the holier will be our walk. May our attitude toward this holy God be like this little boy who, when he refused to do wrong, was teased by his friend with these words, "You are afraid that your dad will hurt you." He aptly replied, "Not really. I am afraid that *I* will hurt him."

That's the mindset of the one who no longer walks in darkness but in the light. We hate sin because sin hurts God. We hate sin not only for what it does to us but primarily for what it does to our loving Savior. So, if there is any sin we need to turn from, let's do so without delay by leaning on the power of the Holy Spirit!

Discussion Questions

1. How has this chapter affected your view of God's holiness?
2. What life changes could you make in light of this attribute of God?
3. How does this attribute of God affect your prayers?
4. How does this attribute of God affect your evangelism?

Scripture Verse for Meditation/Memorization

Exodus 15:11 – *Who among the gods is like you, Lord? Who is like you— majestic in holiness, awesome in glory, working wonders?*

Prayer

Lord, make me as holy as a pardoned sinner can be.[10]

Hymns/Songs

1. "Holy, Holy, Holy" by Reginald Heber
2. "Only a Holy God" by City Alight

---

[10] Robert Murray McCheyne, Gracegems.org.

3. "Revelation Song" by Kari Jobes

4. "Adoration" by John S. B. Monsell, Ken Bible, Tom Fettke

ATTRIBUTE 2

The Power of God

The power of God refers to His ability to do all He plans to do in keeping with His holy character.

David said in Psalm 62:11b, "Power belongs to you, God." Power belongs to God and God alone. The term "Almighty" (Genesis 17:1; Exodus 6:3; 2 Corinthians 6:18; Revelation 1:8) means that God alone possesses all power and authority. It appears over 50 times in the Bible and is used to describe God alone. *Omnipotence,* another word used to describe God being all-powerful, is derived from 2 Latin words: *omni,* meaning all, and *potens,* meaning powerful. In fact, the word "power" is also used as a name of God, as seen in Mark 14:62 when Jesus said to the religious leaders, "You will see the Son of Man sitting at the right hand of the Mighty One" (or "right hand of Power" as in the NASB and ESV). Instead of saying the right hand of God, Jesus states the right hand of the Mighty One or Power, thus implying God and power are inseparable.

God's power is unlike our power. Ours is borrowed power—acquired from outside—from God. God's power is inherent within Himself. He does not have to depend upon others for power or consult with others about how He can or cannot use His power. He is the Almighty!

Stephen Charnock righty said:

> *The power of God is that ability and strength whereby He can bring to pass whatsoever He pleases, whatsoever His infinite wisdom may direct, and whatsoever the infinite purity of His will may resolve…As holiness is the beauty of all God's attributes, so power is that which gives life and action to all the perfections of the divine nature.*
>
> *How vain would be the eternal counsels, if power did not step in to execute them. Without power His mercy would be but feeble pity, His promises an empty sound, His threatenings a mere scarecrow. God's power is like Himself: infinite, eternal, incomprehensible; it can neither be checked, restrained, nor frustrated by the creature.*[11]

So, the question, "Is anything too hard for the LORD?" (Genesis 18:14; Jeremiah 32:27), implies the obvious answer, "Nothing is too hard for you" (Jeremiah 32:17b). Job affirms God's power to do everything with these

---

[11] Quoted in A.W. Pink in *The Attributes of God*, pp. 58-59.

words, "I know that you can do all things; no purpose of yours can be thwarted" (Job 42:2).

There are a couple of things we must understand, though, when studying God's power.

First, even though God *can* do everything, *He will not do anything inconsistent with His holy character.* There are certain self-imposed limitations that God has placed upon Himself. For example, God cannot lie (Titus 1:2, NASB), God cannot be tempted to sin (James 1:13), and He cannot deny Himself (2 Timothy 2:13). God also will not act contrary to His Word. For example, God has not chosen to save all people. Only those who repent from their sins and turn to His Son, Jesus, in faith will be saved. Others will be condemned to hell—no matter how much they plead on the Day of Judgment!

Second, in certain situations, God may choose *not* to show His power. These are not situations that would call for God to compromise His holy character if He displayed His power. Instead, in these situations, God chooses not to show His power for His own reasons. For example, God did not spare His Son from the cross (Romans 8:32). He did not spare many of His children from a cruel death (e.g., Abel in Genesis 4:8 and Stephen in Acts 7:59-60). Could He have shown His delivering power in those situations? Absolutely! However, He did not because it was His plan for these individuals to go through what they went through.

In the same way, at times, you and I will also have to go through certain painful events—not because God lacks the power to deliver us, but because it's just not part of His overall plan. That is what we mean when we say God is sovereign. He exercises His rule over His creation as Sovereign or King. So, we must be careful not to *misquote* verses, such as "With God all things are possible" (Matthew 19:26) as if God will *always* give us a "favorable" result. We must remember that God can and often does exhibit His power to deliver us from trials. Yet there are also certain occasions, in keeping with His purposes, that He does not remove the trial but will keep us secure through it. The latter takes power too!

THE MANIFESTATION OF GOD'S POWER

There are at least eight areas where we see God's power manifested to us as revealed in the Scriptures. Some pertain to the past, some to the present, and others to the future.

1. In Creating the Universe. The Bible opens with this statement: "In the beginning, God created the heavens and the earth" (Genesis 1:1). Right away, we are introduced to God's power. Who can create this entire universe from nothing with just a spoken word? Only God can! The first two chapters of Genesis give us details of the creation events that speak of God's power. Notice the repeated use of the phrase, "And God said" (e.g., Genesis 1:3, 6, 9), and how immediately the appropriate elements of creation came to exist, as seen by the phrase, "And it was so" (Genesis 1:7, 9, 11). That's power—incredible power!

Even without God's special revelation through the Bible, we are told that, according to Romans 1:20, the very creation testifies to God's power. In other words, creation testifies to a Creator. That is why none can give an excuse for denying the existence of God.

2. In Sustaining the Universe. Not only did God create the universe, but He is also the One who sustains it. And that too is accomplished by His powerful word. Hebrews 1:3 states, "The Son is the radiance of God's glory and the exact representation of his being, sustaining all things by his powerful word." Jesus, by His power, sustains the entire universe. In the gospels, we frequently see Jesus' power over nature. Even now, God's power controls the waters from covering the earth. His power even sets limits on disasters, such as earthquakes. It is God's power that sustains human beings as well. God's power sustains a tiny baby in its mother's womb for the entire duration. Not only that, even as adults, it is God's power that sustains us.

3. In Restraining Evil. While God, in His power, will eventually banish all evil from the universe, even now, His power controls evil from running its entire course. Often, we are shocked by events that describe the gruesome acts of evil people. The fact that such actions are not *always* being committed proves that God restrains evil. Human depravity aided by Satanic power can always do much evil (Genesis 6:5; Romans 3:14-18). But, thankfully, God, in His power, has placed restraints. Even when Satan attacked Job, he was still limited by God's power to inflict no more damage than he was allowed (Job 1:12, 2:6).

4. *In Delivering His People.* Events like the Exodus are a clear display of God's mighty power. We are told in Exodus 15:6, "Your right hand, LORD, was majestic in power. Your right hand, LORD, shattered the enemy." The right hand was symbolic of God's great power. Later victories in Canaan under Joshua's leadership and later under David's leadership are clear examples of God's power in delivering His people.

5. *In Conquering Disease and Death.* On numerous occasions during His earthly ministry, the Lord Jesus displayed this power to heal many diseases with a word or a gentle touch. All of that was to show that He was the Messiah, and as the Messiah, when He establishes God's Kingdom with all its glory in the future, there will be no need for anybody to be healed because there will not be any sicknesses to begin with.

However, the most incredible power God displayed was when He raised Jesus from the dead. And by that resurrection, Jesus shows He has the power to conquer disease and death. How so? Disease and death came into this world because of sin (Romans 5:12, 6:23). And since the payment for sins has been fully made, and the resurrection is the proof of it (Romans 4:24-25), one day, both disease and death will also be eliminated entirely (Revelation 21:1-4).

6. *In Changing Lives.* God's power changes human lives as evidenced during all 3 stages of our salvation: justification (of the past), sanctification (in the present), and finally, glorification (in the future).

In Justification. If we are children of God, how did we change from being God-haters to God-lovers? Through the gospel! And the gospel is described by Paul in this manner: "For I am not ashamed of the gospel, because it is the *power* of God that brings salvation to everyone who believes" (Romans 1:16). The gospel *is* the power of God. Through this powerful gospel, God makes people right with Him—an act known as justification. It is through this gospel we receive new life.

In Sanctification. When one becomes a child of God, they also possess that resurrection power through the indwelling presence of the mighty Holy Spirit. That power given to us through the Holy Spirit not only enables us to be witnesses, "you will receive power when the Holy Spirit comes on you; and you will be my witnesses in Jerusalem, and in all Judea and Samaria, and to the ends of the earth" (Acts 1:8), but also enables us to live holy lives, since "His divine power has given us everything we need for a godly life through our knowledge of him who called us by his own glory and goodness" (2 Peter 1:3).

A Christian who once discussed religious matters with a Buddhist asked what he thought about Christianity. The Buddhist replied, "I find a lot of similarities between our teachings. But one thing I find that your faith has which mine does not have is that my faith tells me what I need to do. But it does not give me the power to do it. *Yours gives the power.*"

In Glorification. This refers to the future when we will receive new bodies resembling the body of Jesus. And this new body will be free from sin, suffering, and death. All this will happen when Jesus returns. Philippians 3:20-21 says, "But our citizenship is in heaven. And we eagerly await a Savior from there, the Lord Jesus Christ, who, by the power that enables him to bring everything under his control, will transform our lowly bodies so that they will be like his glorious body."

And in case we doubt if our salvation is secure until this glorification happens, we can be comforted. Peter reminds us that God's power will keep *true* believers secure until they are glorified. We read in 1 Peter 1:5 that we are "shielded by God's power until the coming of the salvation that is ready to be revealed in the last time."

7. *In the Judgment of the Wicked.* Genesis 6–8 reveals the power of God in the past when He judged the wicked world of Noah's time through the universal flood. Revelation 19–20 describes how God, in His power, will one day judge Satan, his demons, and all the unbelievers who have rebelled against Him once and for all. That judgment will result in their being cast into the lake of fire—hell, a place of conscious and everlasting destruction. None will be able to resist His power at that time—just as none could resist His power during the flood in the past. Also, the power of God will be seen in that, even though they will suffer eternal torment in the lake of fire, their bodies will not perish. Why? Because God will give them bodies suitable for hell just like He will give believers bodies ideal for heaven.[12]

8. In Creating a New World. Revelation 21 and 22 describe God's power in destroying this current universe by fire and creating a new heaven and a new earth. It's in this place where we (i.e., all believers) will dwell in the presence of this great God forever and ever.

So, in at least 8 areas God has revealed His power to us. Before I describe how the knowledge of God's power should affect our daily lives, let me say this: Our understanding of God's power is still very, very finite. That great man of God, Job, understood this limitation. That's why, after describing God's incredible power in verses 6-13, he confessed in Job 26:14, "And these are but the outer fringe of his works; how faint the whisper we hear of him! Who then can understand the thunder of his power?" These are just whispers of His power,

---

[12] Revelation 20:12 refers to all the dead unbelievers *standing* before the great white throne on Judgment Day. Jesus Himself, in John 5:29, spoke about those who do evil being *raised* to be condemned. So, unbelievers will also get new bodies suited for hell.

says Job. That's how finite our knowledge is of God's power!

However, a lack of complete knowledge of God's power (and other attributes of His) should not discourage us. We should keep desiring to grow in this knowledge as much as God would help us. And that knowledge should lead to practical application—at least in three specific aspects regarding having this knowledge of God's power.

WE MUST FEAR HIM

We read in Psalm 33:6-7, "By the word of the LORD the heavens were made, their starry host by the breath of his mouth. He gathers the waters of the sea into jars; he puts the deep into storehouses." The following two verses describe what our response should be in the light of God being the all-powerful Creator: "Let all the earth fear the Lord; let all the people of the world revere him. For he spoke, and it came to be; he commanded, and it stood firm" (Psalm 33:8-9). Fear and awe should be the proper response. God is to be feared and revered—not one to be trifled with! *All* His commands are to be obeyed—every one of them without grumbling or questioning.

The reason many unbelievers deny the existence of God is this: By denying, they don't feel the need to be accountable to anyone—especially the One who created them. And if there is no accountability, there will be no fear of judgment. And the result: they feel they can live any way they want! When one denies God as Creator, all other aspects, such as God as Judge and Redeemer, will make no sense. That is why it's essential to start our gospel presentation with God as the Creator (Genesis 1:1), not God as the Judge, Love, or Redeemer. If there is no accountability to the One who made us, then there is no solid foundation to build the good news upon.

WE MUST PRAISE HIM

If we have God on our side (and we do if we are His children), we must constantly praise Him for His power. His mighty hand has delivered us from eternal death to eternal life. He has protected us from His mighty wrath that is to come. He will lead us safely home. And such a truth calls for constant praise and adoration. No wonder Moses sang this song, the first song recorded in the Bible:

> **Exodus 15:11-13** – *Who among the gods is like you, LORD? Who is like you—majestic in holiness, awesome in glory, working wonders? "You stretch out your right hand, and the earth swallows your enemies. In your unfailing love you will lead the people you have redeemed. In your strength you will guide them to your holy dwelling."*

WE MUST TRUST HIM

In Luke 1:37, we read about Gabriel's revelation to Mary that she, as a virgin, would bear the Messiah, "For no word from God will ever fail." Some translations render this verse as, "With God, nothing will be impossible." The idea is that no word or promise from God will ever fail to be fulfilled because nothing or nobody can stop an all-powerful God from accomplishing all His purposes. Mary believed these truths about God. That's why she responded, "I am the Lord's servant…May your *word* to me be fulfilled" (Luke 1:38). She implicitly trusted in God's power to keep His words of promise—no matter what earthly consequences she might face. And God did keep His word even though Mary did face challenges, starting with Joseph initially desiring to break the engagement!

Like Mary, with a humble attitude of trust, we, too, should believe God's power will keep us through life's challenges. And that belief should translate into obeying His commands, no matter the situation. We need to remember that this all-powerful God is also an all-loving God who will never leave or forsake His children (Hebrews 13:5).

Going back to Psalm 62, this time let's look at both verses 11 and 12: "One thing God has spoken, two things I have heard: 'Power belongs to you, God, and with you, Lord, is unfailing love.'" Notice that *love* is accompanied by *power*. Where would we be if we were left only with God's power and no love toward sinners like us? Or where would we be if we were left only with God's love without the power to accomplish the acts of love? Thankfully, both qualities are present in their fullness with God. That's why we must *unflinchingly* trust Him. He promised to be with us and take us home safely. No matter what happens, we can commit our souls to the One who created us and holds us secure in His hands. Let us join David, who said, "In God I trust and am not afraid. What can man do to me?" (Psalm 56:11).

Let's trust Him when He says we have been given the power to overcome every sin, temptation, fear, and addiction and to live a godly life (Romans 6:18; 2 Peter 1:3). And let this trust turn into praise and prayer whereby we continually ask this great God of ours to work this power in our lives through the Holy Spirit so that we can lead a holy life.

If you are not a Christian, imagine having this God unleashing His power against you. How unwise of you to think you can oppose this God and win! Please be warned. There is a judgment coming. How can you escape from this Almighty God? Just like none who mocked God survived the flood during the time of Noah, none who mock God now will escape His coming judgment by fire. Jesus warned in Luke 12:4-5, "I tell you, my friends, do not be afraid of those who kill the body and after that can do no more. But I will show you whom you should fear: Fear him who, after your body has been killed, has authority to throw you into hell. Yes, I tell you, fear him." You can only escape God's judgment by trusting in Jesus. He alone can deliver you from the coming wrath (1 Thessalonians 1:10). Take to heart the severe warning in Psalm 2:12, "Kiss his son, or he will be angry and your way will lead to your destruction, for his wrath can flare up in a moment. Blessed are all who take refuge in him."

Discussion Questions

1. How has this chapter affected your view of God's power?

2. What life changes could you make in light of this attribute of God?

3. How does this attribute of God affect your prayers?

4. How does this attribute of God affect your evangelism?

Scripture Verse for Meditation/Memorization

1 Chronicles 29:11 – *Yours, Lord, is the greatness and the power and the glory and the majesty and the splendor, for everything in heaven and earth is yours. Yours, Lord, is the kingdom; you are exalted as head over all.*

Prayer

Father, You are the omnipotent, the all-powerful God. You reign over all things, including me. Help me to believe and rest in Your delivering power even when there seems to be no way. Protect me from the fear of people. Please help me to fear You more and find rest in the fact that You can provide all that I need. Amen!

Hymns/Songs

1. "A Mighty Fortress Is Our God" by Martin Luther

2. "I Sing the Mighty Power of God" by Isaac Watts

3. "How Great Thou Art" by Stuart K. Hine

4. "Indescribable" by Chris Tomlin

ATTRIBUTE 3

The Presence of God

The presence of God refers to His ability to always be present everywhere with His whole being.

Theologians often describe this attribute of God as the omnipresence of God. It is one of those attributes that reminds us there is no place in this universe where God is not present. Wherever we go, He is there. We cannot hide from Him. We cannot outrun Him, either.

Speaking of outrunning God, did you know that in most of the United States, there is a policy of checking on any stalled vehicle on the highway when temperatures drop to single digits or below? Below is a particular story of when this policy was followed.

Years ago, at about 3:00 a.m. one cold morning, Montana State Trooper Allan Nixon responded to a call about a car off the shoulder of the road outside Great Falls, Montana. He located the car, stuck in the deep snow but with the engine still running.

The trooper walked to the driver's door to find an older man passed out behind the wheel with a nearly empty vodka bottle on the seat beside him. The driver woke up when the trooper tapped on the window. Seeing the rotating lights in his rearview mirror and the state trooper standing next to his car, the man panicked. He jerked the gearshift into "drive" and hit the gas.

The car's speedometer showed 20, 30, 40, and then 50 miles per hour, but it was still stuck in the snow, wheels spinning. The trooper, who had a sense of humor, began running next to the speeding (but stationary) car. The driver lost his mind, thinking the trooper was keeping up with him. This went on for another 30 seconds before the trooper yelled, "PULL OVER!" The man nodded, turned his wheel, and stopped the engine.

Needless to say, the man from North Dakota was arrested and probably shook his head in jail thinking about how the state trooper could outrun him while he was driving 50 miles per hour.[13]

This story reminds us of David's words in Psalm 139:7-12, "Where can I go from your Spirit? Where can I flee

---

[13] https://christianforumsite.com/threads/montana-state-trooper.22329/

from your presence? If I go up to the heavens, you are there; if I make my bed in the depths, you are there. If I rise on the wings of the dawn, if I settle on the far side of the sea, even there your hand will guide me, your right hand will hold me fast. If I say, 'Surely the darkness will hide me and the light become night around me,' even the darkness will not be dark to you; the night will shine like the day, for darkness is as light to you." David stressed there is no place in the entire universe where one could escape the presence of God.

The New Testament declares the same truth as well. In his speech at Athens to the godless philosophers, while urging them to seek God, Paul said, "God ... is not far from any one of us. 'For in him we live and move and have our being'" (Acts 17:27-28a).

So, it is clear from the Bible that God is always present everywhere. The God who is *transcendent* (i.e., high above creation) is also *immanent* (i.e., present among His creation). Isaiah 57:15 pulls both these ideas (transcendence and immanence) together: "For this is what the high and exalted One says—he who lives forever, whose name is holy: 'I live in a high and holy place [i.e., transcendence], but also with the one who is contrite and lowly in spirit, to revive the spirit of the lowly and to revive the heart of the contrite [i.e., immanence].'" Even though He is God seated in the heavens, He is also present among His creation. More importantly, He is also present inside of His children in the person of the Holy Spirit. Amazing truth!

Before we look at how God's omnipresence affects us all in a practical sense, it may be good to briefly address three mistaken ideas about God's omnipresence.

1. Omnipresence does not mean God is present only in part in various places at the same time. God is Spirit and cannot be divided into parts where one part is in one place, and the other parts are in other places. God is present everywhere in His whole being. He is indivisible. God is not contained by space, no matter how vast the space is. Solomon wisely said in 1 Kings 8:27b, "The heavens, even the highest heaven cannot contain you."

In the book *Systematic Theology*, Wayne Grudem writes the following:

> We should guard against thinking that God extends infinitely far in all directions so that he himself exists in a sort of infinite, unending space. Nor should we think that God is somehow a "bigger space" or bigger area surrounding the space of the universe as we know it. All of these ideas continue to think of God's being in spatial terms, as if he were simply an extremely large being. Instead, we should try to avoid thinking of God in terms of size or spatial dimensions. God is a being who exists without size or dimensions in space. In fact, before God created the universe, there was no matter or material so there was no space either. Yet God still existed. Where was God? He was not in a place that we could call a

"where," for there was no "where" or space. But God still was! This fact makes us realize that God relates to space in a far different way than we do or than any created thing does. He exists as a kind of being that is far different and far greater than we can imagine.[14]

2. Omnipresence does not mean God is everything and everything is God. While God is present in every place, this does not necessarily mean every little item has the presence of God in it. That is the idea behind *pantheism*. A pantheist believes that everything is God or He is in everything that exists. However, the Bible says God is present everywhere in His creation, but also *distinct* from His creation.

3. Omnipresence does not mean God is present everywhere in the same sense. For example, we are told in Proverbs 15:29, "The LORD is far from the wicked, but he hears the prayer of the righteous." The statement, "The LORD is far from the wicked," means He is not present to bless them. Their sins have separated God from them (Isaiah 59:2). However, the statement, "he hears the prayer of the righteous," means He is near them to bless them.

Another example would be God's presence in hell, which is different from that in heaven. In hell, God is present to punish the unbeliever (2 Thessalonians 1:9). In heaven, however, He is present to bless the believers (Revelation 21:1-3). So, while it would be wrong to say

---

[14] Second Edition (pp. 207-208). Zondervan Academic. Kindle Edition.

God is more present in one area than in another, it would not be wrong to say that He is present in heaven in a *unique* way—i.e., to bless and show His glory rather than, say, in hell. In other words, God *manifests* His presence more fully in heaven than elsewhere.

With those clarifications about the three common mistaken ideas about God's omnipresence, let's move on to see how this attribute of God is of practical benefit in at least four ways.

1. It Brings Great Joy

In Psalm 16:11, David's response to God's presence was one of great joy: "You make known to me the path of life; you will fill me with joy in your presence, with eternal pleasures at your right hand." While we will experience joy in a complete sense only in the future when we are in heaven, we can experience joy even in our present life as we live in hope for that coming experience of complete joy. When our minds are filled with the truth that we are never alone, that our God, the King of the Universe, is *always* with us both now and forever through all eternity, we will experience great joy, even during great trials. Forgetting this fundamental truth leads to a life that lacks joy and is given to discouragement and anxiety. So, let's make it a habit to remind ourselves that our Heavenly Father is forever with us, His children.

2. It Brings Great Comfort

There's nothing as soothing for the troubled soul as this reminder: God is always with us. That truth helps us obey God even when things are tough, like it helped the believers of the past. Here are some verses that bring out this truth.

> **Psalm 23:4** – *Even though I walk through the darkest valley, I will fear no evil, for you are with me; your rod and your staff, they comfort me.*
>
> **Matthew 28:20** – *And surely I am with you always, to the very end of the age.*
>
> **Acts 18:9-10** – *One night the Lord spoke to Paul in a vision: "Do not be afraid; keep on speaking, do not be silent. For I am with you, and no one is going to attack and harm you, because I have many people in this city."*
>
> **Hebrews 13:5** – *Never will I leave you; never will I forsake you.*

"I am with you even when you walk through the darkest valley—So, don't be afraid" is a constant reminder God gives to His children from Genesis to Revelation! We can recall occasions when we faced intense trials and everything seemed bleak, yet we experienced great peace in our hearts. What was the reason? We, by faith, were able to cling to God's promise that "I am with you always. I will never leave nor forsake you!" Sadly, we can also recall those occasions when, facing intense trials, we were in turmoil. No sleep. Constant fear. What was the reason? We failed to believe in God's promise of never leaving or forsaking us. It was not God's fault. It was ours!

Let's never forget: *Wherever God's will may lead us, His presence will go with us.* It is better to experience His presence in the middle of a jungle than to feel His absence in the middle of a palace! So, if we want to experience comfort during times of trial, we must remember that we are never alone—not even for a second!

3. It Helps Us to Pray Confidently

Knowing that God's presence is always with us gives us a compelling reason to approach Him in prayer. He will hear us because He is always near us. Psalm 145:18 says, "The LORD is near to all who call on him, to all who call on him in truth." This truth should motivate us to say, "Even though I cannot see Him, I *know* He is near me and listening to my cry. So, I will keep on praying!"

4. It Helps Us Resist the Temptation to Sin

Knowing that God is always present is a powerful motivation to resist temptation. It makes us realize that everything we do, everything we even think, including every motive, is done in the presence of God! Proverbs 15:3 says, "The eyes of the LORD are everywhere, keeping watch on the wicked and the good." Proverbs 16:2 says, "All a person's ways seem pure to them, but motives are weighed by the LORD."

You see, typically, we tend to sin when nobody is watching: parents are not watching, the teacher is not watching, our spouse is not watching, friends are not watching, the boss is not watching, and so on. And we become embarrassed if someone catches us doing something wrong. However, if you and I understand and constantly remember that every sin we do, every thought we have, is done right in the presence of a holy God, we will be more prone to resisting sin! One of the secrets of Job's holy life is found in Job 31:4, which says, "Does he not see my ways and count my every step?" He was always aware of God's presence. And that was the reason for His integrity. Like Job, we will be better equipped to resist sin when we realize that God is always present in everything we think or do.

So, there are four benefits when we know that God is always present with us: It brings joy, comfort, helps us to pray confidently, and helps us to resist the temptation to sin. Let us find peace by trusting in this God who is present with us and has promised to help us at all times. Let's continually reflect on verses such as Isaiah 41:10, "So do not fear, for I am with you; do not be dismayed, for I am your God. I will strengthen you and help you; I will uphold you with my righteous right hand."

If you are not a Christian, you might wonder how this knowledge benefits you. Simple. It is a WARNING. God, in His mercy, is warning you to turn from your sinful ways and surrender to Him. You cannot escape from this God who is coming as Judge. You will reap a painful consequence for all eternity if you do not turn from your selfish ways. So, please turn from your sins and turn to Christ. He alone paid the price for sins and rose again. Call out to Him to save you. By faith, surrender to Him as your Lord and Savior. Only then can you receive all the other benefits reserved for the believer we addressed earlier.

Discussion Questions

1. How has this chapter affected your view of God's presence?
2. What life changes could you make in light of this attribute of God?
3. How does this attribute of God affect your prayers?
4. How does this attribute of God affect your evangelism?

Scripture Verse for Meditation/Memorization

Isaiah 41:10 – *So do not fear, for I am with you; do not be dismayed, for I am your God. I will* *strengthen you and help you; I will uphold you with my righteous right hand.*

Prayer

JEHOVAH GOD, Thou Creator, Upholder, Proprietor of all things, I cannot escape from thy presence or control, nor do I desire to do so…

May it keep me from lusting after the world, bear up heart and mind in loss of comforts, enliven me in the valley of death, work in me the image of the heavenly, and give me to enjoy the first fruits of spirituality,

Such as angels and departed saints know.[15]

Amen!

Hymns/Songs

1. "The Lord Is Present Everywhere" by David Ward, Eric Schumacher
2. "Omnipresent God Whose Aid" by Charles Wesley
3. "Lord, Thou Hast Searched Me (Psalm 139)" by Scottish Psalter
4. "Lord, All I Am Is Known to Thee" by Isaac Watts

---

[15] Arthur Bennet, *Valley of Vision*, pp. 106-107.

Attribute 4

The Knowledge of God

The knowledge of God refers to His ability to know all things, actual and possible, past, present, and future in one eternal act.[16]

The knowledge of God, otherwise known as God's *omniscience*, deals with God's all-knowing attribute. In Latin, "omni" means "all," and "science," in its original sense, means "knowledge" or "knowing." Arthur Pink writes:

> God...knows everything: everything possible, everything actual; all events and all creatures, of the past, the present, and the future.[17]

In other words, God does not have to learn anything, nor did He gradually become all-knowing. His knowledge of everything was, is, and always will be perfect (Job 37:16). Nothing catches Him by surprise,

---
[16] Paul Enns, *The Moody Handbook of Theology*, p. 201.
[17] *Attributes of God*, p. 21.

not even the most wicked of acts, and nothing, absolutely nothing, escapes His attention.

God's Knowledge Extends to Actual and Possible Events

God knows what has happened, what will happen, what might have happened, and what might yet happen. In Matthew 11:21, Jesus said, "Woe to you, Chorazin! Woe to you, Bethsaida! For if the miracles that were performed in you had been performed in Tyre and Sidon, they would have repented long ago in sackcloth and ashes." Jesus emphatically stated that Tyre and Sidon would have repented if they had seen the miracles Jesus had done that these people in Chorazin and Bethsaida saw. That is knowledge of what *might* have happened, not mere knowledge of what *did* happen. That's the extent of God's omniscience.

Perhaps the most familiar portion of Scripture that describes God's omniscience is Psalm 139:1-6 and verse 15-16, which says, "You have searched me, LORD, and you know me. You know when I sit and when I rise; you perceive my thoughts from afar. You discern my going out and my lying down; you are familiar with all my ways. Before a word is on my tongue you, LORD, know it completely. You hem me in behind and before, and you lay your hand upon me. Such knowledge is too wonderful for me, too lofty for me to attain…My frame was not hidden from you when I was made in the secret place, when I was woven together in the depths of the earth. Your eyes saw my unformed body;

all the days ordained for me were written in your book before one of them came to be." It is truly beyond our finite understanding to comprehend a God who knows us so intricately!

Not only that, but God also knows all about other creations of His, such as birds and even the stars. Psalm 147:4-5 says, "He determines the number of the stars and calls them each by name. Great is our Lord and mighty in power; his understanding has no limit." Psalm 50:11 says that God "knows every bird in the mountains."

God also knows the future in terms of the events that will happen. Just the fact that so many prophecies have been fulfilled according to their predictions should teach us this fact (e.g., virgin birth as foretold in Isaiah 7:14 and fulfilled in Matthew 1:18-25, and Bethlehem, the place where Jesus would be born as foretold in Micah 5:2 and fulfilled in Luke 2:4-7). These should give us confidence that God will fulfill what He has revealed in many parts of the Bible, including the book of Revelation which speaks about future events, such as the things that "must soon take place" (Revelation 1:1).

THE OMNISCIENCE OF JESUS

Even Jesus exercised this attribute in His earthly ministry, thus displaying His divine nature. In His rebuke to the Pharisees who accused Him of blasphemy for pronouncing forgiveness of sins to a paralyzed man, we read these words, "Knowing their thoughts, Jesus said, 'Why do you entertain evil thoughts in your hearts?'" (Matthew 9:4). Omniscience is reserved only for God; if Jesus knew their thoughts, He is also divine!

But what about Luke 2:52, which says, "And Jesus increased in wisdom and stature, and in favor with God and man?" Why did Jesus have to increase in wisdom if He was already omniscient? The idea of growing in wisdom here refers to Jesus' humanity; He did not yet have full wisdom as a child.

Though Jesus was fully God (John 1:1, 14), when He took on human nature (Philippians 2:6-8), in His humanity, He submitted himself to the normal process of human growth in all areas. Later, even in his public ministry, as the God-Man, Jesus always exercised the use of His divine attributes in accordance with the will of the Father (John 6:38). For example, there were some occasions where His omniscience was on display (Matthew 9:4; John 2:23-25) and on some occasions, it was restricted from being used (Mark 13:32) because that was the Father's will.

The Omniscience of the Holy Spirit

The Holy Spirit is omniscient as well. Paul writes in 1 Corinthians 2:11, "For who knows a person's thoughts except their own spirit within them? In the same way, no one knows the thoughts of God except the Spirit of

God." This statement clearly shows that the Holy Spirit, who knows all God's thoughts, is also divine!

So, **all three persons of the Trinity are omniscient.** They know all things, and nothing is hidden from them. Now, how do these truths benefit believers? In at least four ways.

1. It Leads Us to Praise God More

Even though unbelievers do not like that God is omniscient, believers should be in awe and praise God for this attribute. Truths, such as God knowing all about us right from the womb, knowing all the hairs of our head, knowing what we are thinking, knowing what words come out of our mouths even before they come out, knowing the number of stars, knowing the number of animals, and so on should cause us to join David in praise by saying, "Such knowledge is too wonderful for me, too lofty for me to attain" (Psalm 139:6). We who have our eyes opened to know this awesome God should continually praise Him for His knowledge of everything.

2. It Brings Great Comfort to a Troubled Soul

In trials. In Luke 12:7, Jesus said, "Indeed, the very hairs of your head are all numbered. Don't be afraid; you are worth more than many sparrows." What a comforting thought! Psalm 56:8 reminds us that God even keeps a record of our tears. So, even during great trials, we must not give in to worry because He knows what we are going through.

In failures. Not only in trials does the knowledge of God's omniscience bring comfort, but it also brings comfort when we have sinned and messed up. How so? Remember, God knows everything from beginning to end, even before we were created. So, no sin of ours catches God by surprise, even though it may catch us by surprise.

Psalm 103:14 says that God knows "we are dust." He knows we *will* fail Him at times. And despite knowing we would fail repeatedly, God still set His steadfast love upon us to save and preserve us till the end. That is so comforting! That is why we can freely confess *all* our sins and failures before God and not be shy. He knows our failures anyway. He wants us to come clean in our confession so we can experience His comfort (1 John 1:9). In addition, God does not maintain a record of our sins. Psalm 130:3-4 says, "If you, LORD, kept a record of sins, Lord, who could stand? But with you there is forgiveness, so that we can, with reverence, serve you." Not only does God *not* keep a record of our sins, but He also promises to "remember (our) sins no more" (Hebrews 8:12; Isaiah 43:25) when we become His children. Don't misunderstand. God does not have memory issues when he forgets our sins; it means God will not throw them back in our faces on Judgment Day.

Peter sinned when he denied the Lord three times, but when the resurrected Lord confronted him the third time with the question, "Do you love me?" what was Peter's response? "Lord, you *know* all things; you know that I love you" (John 21:17, emphasis mine). What was the basis of Peter's appeal? The omniscience of Jesus! Put in other words, Peter said, "Lord, You know my heart. Even though I denied You, you are aware that I did it out of fear. Deep inside, You know I love You." That was what he was saying. And the loving Jesus forgave him freely and restored him to the ministry. Now, *that* is comforting!

Sometimes, our hearts condemn us even after we have sought forgiveness for our sins. We beat ourselves up constantly. We must refrain from doing so! Remember the assurance of John, "If our hearts condemn us, we know that God is greater than our hearts, and he knows everything" (1 John 3:20). Take comfort in God's knowledge of all things.

3. It Encourages Us to Pray with Confidence

In Matthew 6:8, in the context of prayer, our Lord Himself encourages us to pray by reminding us of God's omniscience: "Your Father knows what you need before you ask him." Now, some have trouble with prayer because of these very words, wondering that if God knows what we already need, why should we pray? While an all-knowing God ordains the end of all things, He also ordains the means. In other words, prayer is one of the means through which God fulfills what He has already planned. Also, prayer is a way of expressing our dependence upon Him. That's why we can have great confidence when approaching God's throne of grace, knowing He is fully aware of all our needs!

4. It Produces a Greater Sense of Accountability

Proverbs 5:21 says, "For your ways are in full view of the LORD, and he examines all your paths." Proverbs 15:3 says, "The eyes of the LORD are everywhere, keeping watch on the wicked and the good." These verses bring with them a sense of great accountability. *Nothing we think or do is hidden from God's knowledge.*

The Bible goes on further. Not only does God know all our ways, but he also *knows all our motives.* So, it's not just *what* we do that matters, but also the motives, *why* we do it! Paul makes this clear in 1 Corinthians 4:5, "Therefore judge nothing before the appointed time; wait until the Lord comes. He will bring to light what is hidden in darkness and will expose the motives of the heart. At that time, each will receive their praise from God." This verse does not forbid all kinds of judgment but forbids judging the heart motives of others. We don't know the motives of every heart. Only God knows, and He will judge their motives in the future.

For example, we can be:

- Outwardly humble but inwardly proud.

- Outwardly generous but inwardly greedy.
- Outwardly selfless in our service but inwardly seeking to promote our selfish agenda.
- Outwardly loving but inwardly filled with jealousy and hatred.

The list can go on. The bottom line is this: *Mere outward actions do not fool God. He sees the hearts and probes the motives.* We can do something outwardly "Christian," and others may even applaud us. Yet God knows our real motives! That is why it is useless to put on a mask—useless to deliberately practice hypocrisy. God knows the "real" you and me! The opposite applies as well. Even if others criticize us for some action, if our motives are genuinely godly, we can take comfort in that God knows our real motives—even if people are not aware of them. God's perfect knowledge thus brings a greater sense of accountability.

So, there are four benefits the believer can experience from knowing/reflecting on God's omniscience:

1. It leads us to praise God more.
2. It brings great comfort to our troubled souls.
3. It encourages us to pray with confidence.
4. It produces a greater sense of accountability.

However, for the non-Christian, this is one of those attributes, along with the attribute of God's sovereignty (i.e., God doing whatever He chooses to do), that annoys them the most. Why? By nature, we don't want anybody to know more than we want them to know about us, even regarding non-sinful issues. And when it comes to blatantly evil actions, the resistance to this attribute is even greater. For example, adultery is no longer called out as such anymore. Now, it is called a "private affair," meaning it is none of your business. And such thinking also extends toward God: God, don't intrude in my life. What I do is my private business.

Jesus summed up this attitude in clear terms in John 3:19, "This is the verdict: Light has come into the world, but people loved darkness instead of light because their deeds were evil." Sinful humanity does not want their deeds to be exposed: It's my private life. Don't embarrass me or cause me to feel bad about my actions. Just leave me alone. And if anyone brings up God's knowledge of all things and that we must give an account to Him one day, there is tremendous resistance.

This type of attitude is not a new thing. It was present even in Isaiah's day when the righteous confronted the wicked for their sins: "For these are rebellious people, deceitful children, children unwilling to listen to the LORD's instruction. They say to the seers, 'See no more visions!' and to the prophets, 'Give us no more visions of what is right! Tell us pleasant things, prophesy illusions. Leave this way, get off this path, and stop confronting us with the Holy One of Israel!'" (Isaiah

30:9-11). Don't remind us of God. Leave us alone. What we do is our private business. That was their attitude.

You see, it is one thing to love that old popular song by the group Police, which has these lyrics: "Every breath you take, every move you make, every bond you break, every step you take, I'll be watching you." But it is another thing when it comes to God watching *our* every thought and every move! It is a revolting thought. And sinners hate God for being God! But this will not stop an omniscient God from being who He is. He will not bow down to our will or change His ways to accommodate us. He does know everything about us and will call us to account. We cannot escape Him. Hebrews 4:13 says, "Nothing in all creation is hidden from God's sight. Everything is uncovered and laid bare before the eyes of him to whom we must give account." Notice, "everything is uncovered and laid bare" before an all-knowing and all-seeing God!

What we do in the dark, He knows. Psalm 139:11-12 says, "If I say, 'Surely the darkness will hide me and the light become night around me,' even the darkness will not be dark to you; the night will shine like the day, for darkness is as light to you.'" Daniel 2:22 reads, "He reveals deep and hidden things; he knows what lies in darkness, and light dwells with him." When rebuking the evil leaders for "plotting evil" (Ezekiel 11:2), this is what God said, "I know what is going through your mind" (11:5), thereby reminding them of His omniscience.

On the contrary, according to Psalm 10:11b and 13b, the wicked think like this: "God will never notice; he covers his face and never sees...He won't call me to account." But they forget God is watching. Job 34:21 says, "His eyes are on the ways of mortals; he sees their every step." Notice what God Himself has to say about those who live as though He does not see their sins:

> **Numbers 32:23** – *Be sure your sin will find you out.*
>
> **Jeremiah 16:17** – *My eyes are on all their ways; they are not hidden from me, nor is their sin concealed from my eyes."*
>
> **Hosea 7:2** – *But they do not realize that I remember all their evil deeds. Their sins engulf them; they are always before me.*

And one day, this God who sees all things will judge people who have not turned from their sins and turned to Him. These are His solemn words of warning: "I the Lord search the heart and examine the mind, to reward each person according to their conduct, according to what their deeds deserve" (Jeremiah 17:10; also see Revelation 2:23).

The same God who promises to forget the sins of those who have placed their faith in His Son Jesus, who took their punishment for sins, also promises another thing: He *will* remember the sins of those who die without having their sins covered in the blood of His Son Jesus. And He will remember them in a way to bring it to their attention as He pronounces the final judgment—by throwing them into the lake of fire for all eternity.

So, that is the reality that faces those who have never trusted Jesus. God's omniscience will bring all your sins to light. The only way to escape such an end is to turn from your sins and trust in Jesus alone. Will you do it today?

Discussion Questions

1. How has this chapter affected your view of God's knowledge?
2. What life changes would you like to consider in light of this attribute of God?
3. How does this attribute of God affect your prayers?
4. How does this attribute of God affect your evangelism?

Scripture Verse for Meditation/Memorization

Proverbs 5:21 – *For your ways are in full view of the* LORD, *and he examines all your paths.*

Prayer

Lord, You are all-knowing. Nothing is hidden from You. Please help me find comfort in that and, at the same time, remember that truth when I'm tempted. You know my motives, why I do what I do. Protect me from putting on a mask to deceive others and, in that process, fool myself. Please help me to live a life that's clean both on the inside and outside. Amen!

Hymns/Songs

1. "O Lord You Search and Know Me" by Mary Rose Jensen and William W. Walker

2. "The Perfect Wisdom of God" by Stuart Townsend and Keith Getty

3. "O Lord, Thy All Discerning Eyes" by John Quincy Adams

4. "God Omniscient, God All Knowing" by Matt Boswell

Attribute 5

The Fatherhood of God

The Fatherhood of God refers to Him being a Father to everyone who comes to Him through faith in His Son, Jesus Christ.

In his book, *Knowing God*, J.I. Packer wrote the following concerning the Fatherhood of God:

> *If you want to judge how well a person understands Christianity, find out how much he makes of the thought of being God's child, and having God as his Father. If this is not the thought that prompts and controls his worship and prayers and his whole outlook on life, it means he does not understand Christianity very well at all. For everything that Christ taught, everything that makes the New Testament new, and better than the Old, everything that is distinctively Christian as opposed to merely Jewish, is summed up*

in the knowledge of the Fatherhood of God. 'Father' is the Christian name for God.[18]

Since the whole purpose of studying the attributes of God is to grow in our knowledge of Him—because God is known only through His attributes—this knowledge of God as the believer's Father is essential to understanding God better. Hence in this chapter, we will look at God as our Father.

John starts his gospel by describing who Jesus is (John 1:1-5) and the reception He received from the Jewish people as John the Baptist introduced Him (John 1:6-13). While the vast majority rejected Him, a few still put their faith in Him. And to that minority who embraced Jesus, John comforted them with these words of assurance: "Yet to all who did receive him, to those who believed in his name, he gave the right to become children of God" (John 1:12). We are children of God because of our faith in Jesus—that's the promise, that's the real assurance of being able to call God as our Father. And this process through which God makes us His children and thereby enables us to call Him "Father" is what the Bible calls "adoption." Adoption is the highest privilege we can experience—even higher than justification. Let me explain.

Justification occurs right at the moment we receive forgiveness of sins. That is when a guilty sinner standing before a holy God, condemned to die, is freed from sin

---

[18] Quoted in John MacArthur, *God: Coming Face to Face with His Majesty*, p. 126.

Attribute 5: The Fatherhood of God

and guilt due to repenting from sins and placing faith in Jesus Christ. *Justification is foundational to every other blessing because it meets our primary spiritual need.* However, it is not the highest blessing. Why? Justification is a legal term that views God as a Judge. It has to do with our standing before the holy law of God. Adoption, on the other hand, is a family idea. In adoption, "God makes us members of his family."[19] Adoption views God as a Father, thus indicating closeness, affection, and generosity. "To be right with God the Judge is a great thing, but to be loved and cared for by God the Father is far greater."[20] Perhaps the following illustration might help us understand this concept better:

Suppose someone killed your son and is thrown in prison, facing a death sentence. You forgive that man and set him free. That in itself would be a great thing. But you don't stop there. After the killer is released from prison, you now adopt him, make him your own son, and grant him all the privileges that your son would have had! What would that look like? People would even call you insane! But that would show the height of your love and the blessing experienced by the one who killed your precious son.

Is that not the biblical picture of justification and adoption? God could have stopped with justification. But He did not. On top of the blessing of justification, He gave us an even better one—adoption, whereby he

---

[19] Wayne Grudem, *Systematic Theology*, p. 913.
[20] J.I. Packer, *Knowing God*, (London: UK, InterVarsity Christian Fellowship, 1973), p. 253.

makes us His sons and daughters! That is why adoption is a more incredible blessing than justification. And it is through adoption that we see the Fatherhood of God so clearly displayed.

The concept of God as a Father was present even in the Old Testament (Exodus 4:22; Psalm 103:13; Isaiah 64:8). However, in the New Testament, we see the Fatherhood of God in a total sense, seeing that the concept of adoption is more clearly revealed to us. The word translated adoption appears 5 times—all its occurrences appearing in the letters of Paul (Romans 8:15, 23, 9:4; Galatians 4:5; Ephesians 1:5). Paul's readers would have clearly understood this concept because adoption was more common in the New Testament times than in the Old Testament times (though Pharaoh's daughter adopted Moses). In Roman times, it was common practice for the wealthy to adopt young adults whom they saw as fit and could carry on the family name. Many of the Caesars even followed this practice.

However, God's adoption of us is different and higher than human adoption. God has adopted us *not* because He had a need or because He saw something good in us to benefit Him. All He saw in us were rebels who turned our backs on Him. Yet, He adopted us because He simply chose to do so—out of sheer love (Ephesians 1:4-5). Such love is mind-boggling! In John 17:26, Jesus's desire was for the Father to love those who follow Jesus with the same love He has for his Son: "I have made you known to them, and will continue to make you known in order that the love you have for me may be in them and that I myself may be in them." No distinctions in the divine family. We are loved just as Jesus is loved! No wonder the apostle John burst out in praise, "See what great love the Father has lavished on us, that we should be called children of God!" (1 John 3:1).

And such love, which brings about our adoption, results in at least four practical benefits.

1. Adoption Enables Us to Call God Our Father

The term "*Abba*, Father" was used by Jesus when addressing God as His Father (Mark 14:36). Believers can also call Him "*Abba*, Father" (Galatians 4:6) due to the indwelling presence of the Holy Spirit. A glorious new relationship that will last for all eternity has been established. We are loved, well taken care of, and will never be separated from our wonderful Heavenly Father!

2. Adoption Enriches Our Prayer Life

Jesus taught us to address God as "Our Father in heaven" when we pray (Matthew 6:9). This intimacy enables us to approach God our Father with all our requests because He cares for us. We can be free from worry. We can be free from guilt. He forgives all our sins when we confess them. Our loving Father always hears the prayers of His children and answers them according to His good will and pleasure.

3. Adoption Strengthens Our Hope for the Future

Paul tells us in Romans 8:23b that "we wait eagerly for our adoption to sonship, the redemption of our bodies." He went on to say, "For in this hope we were saved. But hope that is seen is no hope at all. Who hopes for what they already have? But if we hope for what we do not yet have, we wait for it patiently" (Romans 8:24-25). In essence, Paul was saying that the fullest experience of adoption that will come is when we receive glorified bodies. This truth should fill us with steadfast hope to endure the trials of this present life. According to 2 Corinthians 1:22b, God has placed "his Spirit in our hearts as a deposit, guaranteeing what is to come." The phrase "guaranteeing what is to come" refers to the fact that in the future, we will be with the Lord in our glorified state for all eternity. This truth also strengthens our hope.

4. Adoption Enables Us to Be Trained by God

Hebrews 12:5b-6 says, "My son, do not make light of the Lord's discipline, and do not lose heart when he rebukes you, because the Lord disciplines the one he loves, and he chastens everyone he accepts as his son." The writer goes on to mention, "Endure hardship as discipline; God is treating you as his children"

(Hebrews 12:7). In essence, the writer of Hebrews says that *because* we are God's children, God disciplines us. And that's a good thing! It shows we are His children! The end goal of this disciplining process is stated in Hebrews 12:10: "In order that we may share in his holiness."

In light of these four benefits of adoption (and more could be added), what should be our response? Simple. We are to "imitate God our Father." If we are his sons and daughters, we should display family resemblance! And that means we are to pursue holiness since God is holy (1 Peter 1:15-16). We are to love as God loves (Ephesians 5:1-2), with a love that extends even to our enemies (Matthew 5:44-45). God's children should never forget that we are one family. That's why there's no room for bitterness, jealousy, and fighting. We share each other's joys and sorrows. What a loving Father we have in God. And what a glorious future we have! I trust these truths would strengthen our holy resolve to imitate our Father!

If you are not God's child and still cannot call Him your Father, today would be a good day to settle that issue. You can be adopted into His family by turning from your sins and embracing Christ as your Lord and Savior. Once again, let me remind you of John 1:12, "Yet to all who did receive him, to those who believed in his name, he gave the right to become children of God." When you put your faith in Jesus, you will be welcomed into God's family as His son or daughter.

And then you also can enjoy all these benefits of adoption! Don't hesitate. Please come. God *always* has room in His family for more children! Human fathers have weaknesses, and they often fail. However, the one and only Heavenly Father—the Father of the Lord Jesus Christ has no weaknesses. He will never forget or fail you. He will love you with perfect love for all eternity!

Discussion Questions

1. How has this chapter affected your view of God being a Father to all who place their faith in Jesus?

2. What life changes could you make in light of this attribute of God?

3. How does this attribute of God affect your prayers?

4. How does this attribute of God affect your evangelism?

Scripture Verse for Meditation/Memorization

Romans 8:15 – *The Spirit you received does not make you slaves, so that you live in fear again; rather, the Spirit you received brought about your adoption to sonship. And by him we cry, "Abba, Father."*

Prayer

Father, what a privilege You have given to us to call You our Heavenly Father. Thank You for this intimacy. Help us to live like Your children just as our Lord and Savior Jesus lived. Please give us a spirit of humility to accept those times when You discipline us. Help us remember You discipline all whom You love and that You do it for our good and Your glory. Amen!

Hymns/Songs

1. "Our Father Exalted" by Ken Bible
2. "How Deep the Father's Love" by Stuart Townsend
3. "A Child of the King" by Harriett E. Buell
4. "Father God I Wonder" by Kate Miner

ATTRIBUTE 6

The Love of God

The love of God refers to Him giving "Himself and His gifts spontaneously, voluntarily, righteously, and eternally, for the good of personal beings regardless of their merit or response."[21]

God's love or the love of God is the most known and often discussed among God's attributes. We read in 1 John 4:8, "God is love." The same is repeated later in 1 John 4:16 as well. Note carefully that it does not say God has love but that God *is* love. Love is not merely one of God's attributes. Instead, love is the very nature of God. God's other attributes, such as mercy, goodness, patience, and grace, closely relate to love since they arise from God's love. The more we understand His love, the more our troubled hearts will experience peace, and the more our love for Him and others will increase. To achieve that goal, we will look

---

[21] Rolland McCune, *Systematic Theology, Volume 1* (Allen Park: MI, Detroit Baptist Theological Seminary), p. 255.

at four key characteristics of God's love in this chapter and then draw practical applications for our lives.

CHARACTERISTIC #1: GOD'S LOVE IS A VOLUNTARY LOVE

God was and is under no compulsion to love us. He didn't set His love upon us because we were worthy of being loved. In truth, it is the exact opposite. We are unworthy people who have sinned greatly against Him. Yet God, on His own, *uninfluenced* by any external factors, has set His love upon us. We read in 1 John 4:10, "This is love: not that we loved God, but that he loved us." Later, we read in 1 John 4:19, "We love because he first loved us."

God's voluntary love is not just a New Testament concept. We see this truth stated even in the Old Testament. In Deuteronomy 7:7-8, God describes His covenant love for Israel as *not* being based on Israel's worthiness but based on His voluntary choice: "The LORD did not set his affection on you and choose you because you were more numerous than other peoples, for you were the fewest of all peoples. But it was because the LORD loved you and kept the oath he swore to your ancestors that he brought you out with a mighty hand and redeemed you from the land of slavery, from the power of Pharaoh king of Egypt." Simply stated, God loved Israel because He *chose* to love them.

Characteristic #2: God's Love Is a Holy Love

God's love does not cancel His holiness. That "God is love" (1 John 4:8) does not diminish or deny the other attributes of God, such as "God is light" (1 John 1:5) or that "God is a righteous judge" (Psalm 7:11). Even in the famous John 3:16 passage, God loved the world in a manner that included the provision of an atonement for sin, as indicated by the phrase, "He gave his one and only Son." God's love is holy, which means He cannot take sin lightly—even in the life of His children. That is why Hebrews 12:6 states, "The Lord disciplines the one he loves, and he chastens everyone he accepts as his son." That kind of discipline may sometimes involve sickness and even death (1 Corinthians 11:30)! A holy love cannot and will not wink at sin.

The newspapers once carried the story of a father and mother who, finding that their little girl had taken and eaten something from the cupboard, began to shake and slap the child. When the child became drowsy, they did not let up, but continued shaking and slapping her for four hours. What seemed like a cruel punishment for such a minor offense was, in all reality, compelled by love. The child had swallowed ten sleeping tablets, and the doctor said that the only hope of saving the child's life was to keep her awake.

Similarly, we do not always understand the path down which God leads us, but we may be sure His chastisement is always born of love. God does not choose to stop the harshness of the winds but instead directs and carries us through them.

Characteristic #3: God's Love Is a SACRIFICIAL Love

God's love gives even when the cost is exceptionally high. Human love is often characterized by lofty words but empty actions, as seen by great promises made on the wedding day that are sadly followed by bitter divorce months or years later. When a sacrifice is to be made, human love, for the most part, collapses.

God's love, however, is not so. It is sacrificial. The supreme example of God's sacrificial love is nowhere seen more clearly than at the cross. Here is where God gave sinners like you and me his very best—His One and only Son—the Lord Jesus Christ as read in Romans 5:6-8, "You see, at just the right time, when we were still powerless, Christ died for the ungodly. Very rarely will anyone die for a righteous person, though for a good person someone might possibly dare to die. But God demonstrates his own love for us in this: While we were still sinners, Christ died for us." And how can we forget the very familiar words of John 3:16, "For God so loved the world that he gave his one and only Son, that whoever believes in him shall not perish but have eternal life."

A story is told of a young man in France who was greatly loved by his mother. However, he pursued a very sinful way of life. He became very attracted to a wicked woman who dragged him further and further into sin. The loving mother tried to draw him back from sin, which caused the woman to hate the mother. One night, the woman got the young man drunk and accused him of not truly loving her. He promised that he did. She said that if he truly loved her, he would get rid of his mother, who was trying to separate him from her.

The story went on to say that the young man rushed from the woman's home and went to his house where his mother was asleep. In an act of great cruelty, he beat his mother to death and then went on to tear out her heart and bring it to his lover. As he ran to his lover's home with the bleeding heart of his mother, he tripped over a stone, stumbled, and fell. Immediately, the bleeding heart cried, "My son, are you hurt?"

That's the kind of sacrificial love God displays for terrible sinners such as you and me. Anytime we are tempted to doubt God's love, we must look at the cross and repeatedly be reminded how much God loves us. Will He who did not withhold His Son for our sake forget us (Romans 8:32)? Will He abandon us? Never!

Characteristic #4: God's Love Is an EVERLASTING Love

Human love is often based on sentimental feelings which go up and down. When my emotions are up, I will love you. When I feel down, I will distance myself from you. If you love me and never disappoint me, I will love you. If not, I cannot love you.

God's love, however, is not so. He does not change His mind. His love endures forever. He loved us even before the heavens were created (Ephesians 1:4-5). And His love will eternally extend even after the new heavens and new earth are created. It is an everlasting love, as God Himself declares through Jeremiah, "I have loved you with an everlasting love; I have drawn you with unfailing kindness" (Jeremiah 31:3). While this verse primarily refers to God's everlasting, electing, covenant love to Israel, we can legitimately apply it to all believers of all ages. In Romans 8:38-39, Paul said, "For I am convinced that neither death nor life, neither angels nor demons, neither the present nor the future, nor any powers, neither height nor depth, nor anything else in all creation, will be able to separate us from the love of God that is in Christ Jesus our Lord." Paul asked the question of whether anything on earth can separate us from God's love (Romans 8:35a), and he answered that question with a resounding *no* by listing all possible forces that can't create such a separation—which is everything (Romans 8:35b-39).

Indeed, His love is everlasting. What a comforting thought! Even if all the world—including our nearest and dearest ones hate and reject us, we can be comforted. The King of the universe who made us and sent His Son to die for us will never stop loving us. He will never hate or disown us—even when we fail miserably. Peter failed miserably by denying Jesus three times. Yet, Jesus came personally to him and assured him of His love (John 21:15-17). Even when we go through intense trials, and it feels like God is distant or has just forgotten us, we don't need to lose heart. God has loved us with an everlasting love.

So, we've seen four beautiful characteristics of God's love: it is voluntary, holy, sacrificial, and everlasting. What are the implications of gaining this knowledge? There are two in particular: *Our love for God and our love for neighbors should increase.*

In Matthew 22:37-39, Jesus taught us the two most important commandments: "'Love the Lord your God with all your heart and with all your soul and with all your mind.' This is the first and greatest commandment. And the second is like it: 'Love your neighbor as yourself.'" Let's briefly see how this can happen in practical ways.

1. Our Love for God Should Increase

Our love for God should increase in practical areas such as the following:

Praise. Notice how John burst forth in praise as he reflected on God's love: "See what great love the Father has lavished on us, that we should be called children of God! And that is what we are!" (1 John 3:1). We must constantly praise Him for loving us without compromising His holy nature. We must not grumble or be angry at Him when He disciplines us. It is for our good. His holy love teaches us to pursue holiness in all that we think and do.

Purity. Notice how John also calls us to pursue purity: "All who have this hope in him purify themselves, just as he is pure" (1 John 3:3). How can we hurt Him who has loved us despite our wretchedness?

Scriptures and Prayer. We also express our love for God by spending time reading the Bible (hearing from Him) and in prayer (talking to Him).

Sacrificial Giving. God's sacrificial love, whereby He gave us His very best, demands that we never withhold anything from being used for God's purposes. Our money, our time, and our possessions all belong to God. We must ask ourselves: Does giving my time and money for God's purposes include a *sacrificial* element? If not, we must repent and respond rightly. David said in 2 Samuel 24:24, "I will not sacrifice to the LORD my God burnt offerings that cost me nothing." When we love someone, we will not count the cost. Mary did not calculate the cost when she poured the expensive perfume on Jesus (John 12:3). Why? She was moved by Jesus' love for her and, in response, sacrificially expressed her love for Him.

Ongoing Trust. We must continue to trust Him—even when things seem dark. He who perseveres in His love for us deserves the same from us.

2. Our Love for Our Neighbors Should Increase

Ephesians 5:1-2 says, "Follow [or imitate] God's example, therefore, as dearly loved children and walk in the way of love, just as Christ loved us and gave himself up for us as a fragrant offering and sacrifice to God." And then in 1 John 4:11-12, we read, "Dear friends, since God so loved us, we also ought to love one another. No one has ever seen God; but if we love one another, God lives in us and his love is made complete in us."

Here are some ways we can imitate God's love through our love for our neighbors.

Voluntary Love. Just as God's love toward us was not based on our worthiness, our love for others should be the same. We should be willing to love others no matter what color they are, what language they speak, how educated they are, how much wealth they might possess, or how bad they might be.

Holy Love. We read in 1 Corinthians 13:6, "Love does not delight in evil but rejoices with the truth." If we are to imitate God's love in this particular manner, our love for others should not cause us to be indifferent or silent about their sins. We should, in love, warn them. Also, we must not do anything that would harm them either. Our words to others should be loving and kind. We must always speak words that build others—not tear them down. It means no lying, gossip, slander, or sinful speech (Ephesians 4:29). It also means not being a stumbling block to them by our actions (1 Corinthians 10:31-33).

Sacrificial Love. John makes it clear how we should respond in light of such sacrificial love in 1 John 3:16: "This is how we know what love is: Jesus Christ laid down his life for us. And we ought to lay down our lives for our brothers and sisters." John then goes on to give an example of how this sacrificial love can be expressed in a practical sense in verses 17 and 18: "If anyone has material possessions and sees a brother or sister in need but has no pity on them, how can the love of God be in that person? Dear children, let us not love with words or speech but with actions and in truth."

Everlasting Love. Since God does not stop loving us when we fail Him, we, too, cannot stop loving people when they fail us. We are reminded in 1 Corinthians 13:4 and 7, "Love is patient, love is kind…[love] always hopes, perseveres." Is our love like that? Is there anybody with whom we are cold in our love? Then, we need to set it right. Realizing that we are loved with everlasting love should motivate us to love others similarly.

A greater understanding of God's love should *always* lead us to a greater love for our neighbors, including telling the lost people around us about God's love as expressed through Christ. Loving God and loving others are inseparable evidence of a truly changed heart. Where love for either is missing, the work of the Holy Spirit is missing, thus indicating one is not saved. That is what God's Word declares in 1 John 4:20, "Whoever claims to love God yet hates a brother or sister is a liar. For whoever does not love their brother and sister, whom they have seen, cannot love God, whom they have not seen."

This supernatural power to love others—including our enemies is an authentic proof that the Holy Spirit indwells us, thus indicating we are children of God (John 13:34-35). We are called to resemble the God who is love. So, we need to ask Him to teach and energize us through the Holy Spirit to love Him and others with a love similar to His love for us.

If you are not yet a Christian, I urge you to accept the loving offer that God gives to you to embrace His Son, Jesus Christ, who was crucified for your sins and was raised again for the forgiveness of your sins. You don't know what true love is until you have tasted the love of God offered through Jesus Christ. Jesus Himself lovingly invites you through these words:

> **Matthew 11:28-30** – *Come to me, all you who are weary and burdened, and I will give you rest. Take my yoke upon you and learn from me, for I am gentle and humble in heart, and you will find rest for your souls. For my yoke is easy and my burden is light.*

In case you are hesitant to accept His invitation to come to Him because you feel you have sinned much and doubt if Jesus will ever accept you, allow me to remind you of Jesus's loving words of assurance: "Whoever comes to me I will *never* drive away" (John 6:37b). So, without delay, please come to Him and taste His everlasting love. David said in Psalm 34:8, "Taste and see that the LORD is good; blessed is the one who takes refuge in him." If you reject this loving invitation from God, the time will come when you will never ever be able to know what love is for all eternity! All you will be left to consciously experience for all eternity is God's terrible wrath.

DISCUSSION QUESTIONS

1. How has this chapter affected your view of God's love?

2. What life changes could you make in light of this attribute of God?

3. How does this attribute of God affect your prayers?

4. How does this attribute of God affect your evangelism?

SCRIPTURE VERSE FOR MEDITATION/MEMORIZATION

Jeremiah 31:3 – *I have loved you with an everlasting love; I have drawn you with unfailing kindness.*

Attribute 6: The Love of God

PRAYER

> GRACIOUS LORD,
> Thy name is love,
> In love receive my prayer.
> My sins are more than the wide sea's sand,
> But where sin abounds,
> There is grace more abundant.
> Look to the cross of thy beloved Son,
> and view the preciousness of his atoning blood;
> Listen to his never-failing intercession,
> and whisper to my heart, 'Thy sins are forgiven,
> be of good cheer, lie down in peace.'...
> Unsought, thou hast given me
> the greatest gift, the person of they Son,
> and in him thou wilt give me all I need.[22]
> Amen!

HYMNS/SONGS

1. "The Love of God" by Frederick H. Lehman
2. "Love of God" by Stuart Townsend and Keith Getty
3. "And Can It Be" by Charles Wesley
4. "O Love That Wilt Not Let Me Go" by George Matheson

---

[22] Arthur Bennet, *Valley of Vision*, pp. 270-271.

Attribute 7

The Wisdom of God

The wisdom of God refers to His ability to know all things and choose the best and highest goals and the best means to achieve those goals in order to glorify Himself the most.

The wisdom of God is also known as the *omnisapience* of God (In Latin, *omni* means "all" and *sapient* means "wise"). In the conclusion of his letter to the Romans, the Apostle Paul writes, "To the only wise God be glory forever through Jesus Christ! Amen" (Romans 16:27). Did you notice how he described God as the "only wise God"? Earlier in Romans 11:33, Paul praised God for His wisdom and knowledge in this manner: "Oh, the depth of the riches of the wisdom [omnisapience] and knowledge [omniscience] of God! How unsearchable his judgments, and his paths beyond tracing out!"

While we can never fully comprehend this attribute of God, let alone any other attribute of His, we will try to better understand it by asking and answering four questions:

1. What is the wisdom of God?
2. How does God display His wisdom?
3. How does God communicate His wisdom to us?
4. How can we know if we are growing in God's wisdom?

1. What Is the Wisdom of God?

Knowledge refers to what one knows. Wisdom refers to the application of that knowledge. In the Bible, wisdom has an intellectual and moral quality to it. So, when the Bible describes God as wise, this is what it's saying: An all-knowing (the intellectual side) God has the ability to choose the best and highest goals (the moral side) and the best means (the moral side) to achieve those goals in order to glorify Himself the most.

In other words, the wisdom of God is the practical side of God's knowledge, which, when applied, achieves His desires in ways that will glorify Him the most. And whatever God, in His wisdom, has chosen to accomplish, He will do it because He has the power to do so. Remember, God is omnipotent. He has all power, as we saw in the chapter "The Power of God." That is why Scripture often links the wisdom of God with the power of God. Here are specific examples:

Job 9:4 – *His wisdom is profound, his power is vast. Who has resisted him and come out unscathed?*

Daniel 2:20 – *Praise be to the name of God for ever and ever; wisdom and power are his.*

Romans 16:25, 27 – *Now to him who is able to establish you [signifies power] in accordance with my gospel, the message I proclaim about Jesus Christ, in keeping with the revelation of the mystery hidden for long ages past…to the only wise God be glory forever through Jesus Christ! Amen.*

So, the wisdom of God is an all-knowing God with the ability (or power) to choose the best and highest goals and the best means to achieve those goals in order to glorify Himself the most!

2. How Does God Display His Wisdom?

We can see God's wisdom displayed in at least four areas.

In Creation. We read in Psalm 104:24, "How many are your works, Lord! In wisdom you made them all; the earth is full of your creatures." The arrangement of the entire universe and the unique way our bodies are created clearly display God's wisdom.

In Redemption. We read in 1 Corinthians 1:18 and verse 25 these words, "For the message of the cross is foolishness to those who are perishing, but to us who are being saved it is the power of God...For the foolishness of God is wiser than human wisdom, and the weakness of God is stronger than human strength." In these verses, Paul essentially says that the message of the cross is foolishness to those who do not believe (i.e., the "wise" of the world). Who would think of such a way to save people? Yet, to those who believe, they understand the wisdom of God through this message. God accomplishes His saving work in this way (i.e., through preaching about the cross) so that "no one may boast before him" (1 Corinthians 1:29)!

In the Church. When Paul preached the gospel to both the Jews and Gentiles, upon believing, both these groups that had been racially divided for centuries became one unified body in Christ. Ephesians 3:6 says, "This mystery is that through the gospel the Gentiles are heirs together with Israel, members together of one body, and sharers together in the promise in Christ Jesus." By bringing both these groups together, God fulfilled His purpose: "His intent was now, through the church, the manifold wisdom of God should be made known to the rulers and authorities in the heavenly realms, according to his eternal purpose that he accomplished in Christ Jesus our Lord" (Ephesians 3:10-11). For example, even angels and demons see the power of people from different racial, cultural, and economic backgrounds when they come together as one body in Christ. And that profoundly reveals God's wisdom and ultimately brings glory to Him.

In the Lives of Believers. When God created the entire universe, including humans, He desired to be glorified and honored through them. We are told in Revelation 4:11, "You are worthy, our Lord and God, to receive glory and honor and power, for you created all things, and by your will they were created and have their being." Stated differently, we were created to have God as our sole treasure and object of love. Loving Him with all of our hearts and minds and strength is the purpose of our existence.

However, due to the entrance of sin and its devastating effects, this purpose has been hindered—for a time! However, through the gospel, God is working on bringing all things to Himself to achieve that original goal of all creation glorifying and honoring Him as He rightly deserves. Included in that goal is the formation of a people for Himself who will love, cherish, and honor Him above all things: the people known as His children—that includes us, both you and me! And that goal will be fully realized when we are all made like Jesus Christ. That is His goal for the believer. Here are a few texts that highlight this marvelous truth.

> **Romans 8:28-29** – *And we know that in all things God works for the good of those who love him, who have been called according to his purpose. For those God foreknew he also predestined to be conformed to the image of his Son, that he might be the firstborn among many brothers and sisters.*

> **1 Corinthians 15:49** – *And just as we have borne the image of the earthly man, so shall we bear the image of the heavenly man.*
>
> **Philippians 3:20-21** – *But our citizenship is in heaven. And we eagerly await a Savior from there, the Lord Jesus Christ, who, by the power that enables him to bring everything under his control, will transform our lowly bodies so that they will be like his glorious body.*

So, God is working all events, both the joys and the sufferings in our lives, to bring us to the fulfillment of that ultimate reality: to be like His Son! But when we fail to understand this truth, we will not gladly embrace His will—especially when we face trials! We must remember that even Jesus was not exempt from suffering (Hebrews 2:10). And we are called to walk in His footsteps (1 John 2:6)! That is why we must not lose focus when suffering comes. We should respond like Paul did, even in the face of unrelenting trials, by resting in God's grace (2 Corinthians 12:7-10). We must trust and yield to God's ways because, through ALL our life situations, an all-wise God seeks to glorify Himself by molding us into the image of Christ.

3. How Does God Communicate His Wisdom to Us?

Some of God's attributes are incommunicable (e.g., omnipotence, omniscience, eternity, etc.). However, wisdom is a communicable attribute. How do we

Attribute 7: The Wisdom of God

know this? Because the Bible says so! Numerous commands in the Bible call for us to grow in wisdom. The majority of the book of Proverbs supports this truth.

> **Proverbs 1:1-2** – *The proverbs of Solomon son of David, king of Israel: for gaining wisdom and instruction; for understanding words of insight.*

> **Proverbs 4:5** – *Get wisdom, get understanding; do not forget my words or turn away from them.*

> **Proverbs 5:1** – *My son, pay attention to my wisdom, turn your ear to my words of insight.*

Not only Proverbs, but other books in the Bible also mention this same idea.

> **Matthew 10:16b** – *Be as shrewd as snakes and as innocent as doves.*

> **Ephesians 5:15** – *Be very careful, then, how you live—not as unwise but as wise.*

From these Scriptures, it is clear that God wants to impart wisdom to us. So, how do we receive it?

Firstly, we must realize our need for wisdom. What we have that we boast as wisdom (i.e., human wisdom) is foolishness before God. We must humbly recognize we don't have the wisdom the Bible describes as true wisdom. We should, like Agur, confess this to God: "Surely I am only a brute, not a man; I do not have human understanding. I have not learned wisdom, nor have I attained to the knowledge of the Holy One" (Proverbs 30:2-3).

Secondly, we must realize God will give wisdom to those who ask Him. Proverbs 2:6 assures us, "For the Lord gives wisdom; from his mouth come knowledge and understanding." No wonder Paul frequently prayed for wisdom in the lives of other believers in his letters (Philippians 1:9-11; Colossians 1:9). However, when we ask, our asking should be marked with these four attitudes:

1. Fear of the Lord (Psalm 11:10; Proverbs 1:7, 9:10).
2. Persistence (Proverbs 2:1-6).
3. Humility (Proverbs 11:2).
4. Faith (James 1:5, especially in the context of trials).

Thirdly, we must realize God gives it through His Word. Scriptures alone reveal how we can be saved (2 Timothy 3:15) and how we can be sanctified (i.e., grow in holiness) (2 Timothy 3:16; John 17:17; Acts 20:32; Deuteronomy 4:5-8; Psalm 19:7, 119:11). That is why Jesus said we "shall not live on bread alone, but on every word that comes from the mouth of God" (Matthew 4:4). Sadly, today, most professing believers live by social media, television, or other means, instead of directly taking in the Scriptures. One cannot grow in true wisdom apart from the Scriptures! It is the Word, as applied by the Holy Spirit that God uses to help us grow in wisdom and understanding. Of course, mere knowledge will not be of use. We must obey what God teaches us. If not, we are deceiving ourselves (James 1:22)!

When these three attitudes mentioned above mark our asking, we can be *sure* God will give wisdom to us. Why? Because such a desire indicates that we seek to apply that wisdom so that we will glorify God and not ourselves! And we can be confident that such an attitude pleases God, and God *will* pour out His wisdom to such hearts.

4. How Can We Know If We Are Growing in God's Wisdom?

James 3:13-18 is a good test:

> *Who is wise and understanding among you? Let them show it by their good life, by deeds done in the humility that comes from wisdom. But if you harbor bitter envy and selfish ambition in your hearts, do not boast about it or deny the truth. Such "wisdom" does not come down from heaven but is earthly, unspiritual, demonic. For where you have envy and selfish ambition, there you find disorder and every evil practice. But the wisdom that comes from heaven is first of all pure; then peace-loving, considerate, submissive, full of mercy and good fruit, impartial and sincere. Peacemakers who sow in peace reap a harvest of righteousness.*

How does our life match with what James is saying? The answer will tell each of us if we are growing or not.

So, four questions about wisdom were asked and answered:

1. What is the wisdom of God?
2. How does God display His wisdom?
3. How does God communicate His wisdom to us?
4. How can we know if we are growing in God's wisdom?

As I said earlier, Paul told us we can never fully understand God's ways. They are beyond our understanding (Romans 11:33). Even in the Old Testament, God made it clear to us through Isaiah: "'For my thoughts are not your thoughts, neither are your ways my ways,' declares the Lord. 'As the heavens are higher than the earth, so are my ways higher than your ways and my thoughts than your thoughts'" (Isaiah 55:8-9). Yes, there will always be times when we cannot understand why certain events happened to us or did not happen. It may seem hard to understand and follow God's commands during those occasions. What should be our response at such times? Here are some answers from the Scriptures:

> **Proverbs 3:5-6** – *Trust in the Lord with all your heart and lean not on your own understanding; in all your ways submit to him, and he will make your paths straight.*

Attribute 7: The Wisdom of God

1 Peter 4:19 – *So then, those who suffer according to God's will should commit themselves to their faithful Creator and continue to do good.*

Dear fellow brother and sister in Christ, remember, God's ultimate goal for you and me is to bring us to a state where we will be like His Son and, thereby, please Him fully. We'll have difficulty yielding to His will when we forget this truth. However, embracing it wholeheartedly will result in a life that is not only joyful but also one that continually and in an increasing measure keeps bringing glory to God.

Dear non-Christian friend, if you are not a believer or just playing the game of being a Christian, please remember that your wisdom is foolishness before God (Romans 1:21). You need to turn to God's wisdom as displayed on the cross. You need to turn from your ways of trying to please God and turn to His way. And that is by looking to His Son, Jesus, who lived the perfect life (which you cannot live even for one second), died on the cross, and rose again. Come to Jesus "in whom are hidden all the treasures of wisdom and knowledge" (Colossians 2:3). Place your faith in Him and follow Him. That is the wisest thing you can ever do!

Discussion Questions

1. How has this chapter affected your view of God's wisdom?

2. What life changes could you make in light of this attribute of God?

3. How does this attribute of God affect your prayers?

4. How does this attribute of God affect your evangelism?

Scripture Verse for Meditation/Memorization

Romans 11:33 – *Oh, the depth of the riches of the wisdom and knowledge of God! How unsearchable his judgments, and his paths beyond tracing out!*

Prayer

Father, You are the all-wise God. In wisdom, You have created all things. You have planned every step of my life from start to finish. How foolish of me that I often think and act as if my ways are better than Yours. Protect me from pursuing my own ways, Father. Help me to trust in Your wisdom and ways as You reveal through the Scriptures, even if that leads me to challenging paths. Please guide and help me to please You in all my ways.

Amen!

Hymns/Songs

1. "The Perfect Wisdom of Our God" by Stuart Townsend and Keith Getty
2. "Immortal Invisible God Only Wise" by Walter C. Smith
3. "God Moves in a Mysterious Way" by William Cowper
4. "In All Thy wisdom, Father God" by Witness Lee

ATTRIBUTE 8

The Wrath of God

The wrath of God refers to His eternal and holy hatred of all sin, resulting in Him punishing it.

One of the most neglected teachings of the Church and of many professing Christians is the truth about God's wrath. Even the mention of this attribute is repulsive to many. And when forced to deal with God's wrath, there's a tendency to do it apologetically, almost like saying, "I'm sorry the Bible describes God as being a God of wrath."

Often, the reason for such a negative attitude is people's difficulty in reconciling a God of love also being a God of wrath. They wrestle with the thought, "How could a loving and merciful God also be a punishing God?" Such thinking is due to a faulty view of God that arises from a lack of proper understanding of what the Bible says about God's attributes as a whole. Typically, when we use the word "wrath," the first thing that comes to mind for many is a maniac running around with a gun and shooting people indiscriminately. They tend to view God in the same light as someone who arbitrarily kills or inflicts pain on people simply because He lost His temper. Nothing is farther from the truth. Unlike sinful human anger, God's wrath is in keeping with His holy nature.

God is holy. And sin—every kind of sin—opposes the holy nature of God. Stated in another way: sin is everything opposite of who God is. How can a sovereign God tolerate anything that opposes Him and yet stay sovereign? No, God must punish sin in keeping with His holy and righteous character. Imagine a holy God who did not hate sin or was even troubled by it. Can we fully praise Him for being a righteous God without any reservation? Indeed, we cannot!

Therefore, we should not view the wrath of God as a negative attribute or as something that stands in opposition to His other attributes, such as love, mercy, kindness, and goodness. God is the sum of all perfections. While God can love perfectly, He can also hate perfectly all that is opposed to what is good—namely evil. God cannot be perfect if He does not deal with sin. That is why it should not surprise us that the Bible frequently talks about God's wrath. In fact, God Himself describes His wrath in vivid terms without any shame or apologies:

> **Deuteronomy 32:39-41** – *There is no god besides me. I put to death and I bring to life, I have wounded and I will heal, and no one can deliver*

out of my hand. See I lift my hand to heaven and solemnly swear: As surely as I live forever, See when I sharpen my flashing sword and my hand grasps it in judgment, I will take vengeance on my adversaries and repay those who hate me.

He who delights in all that is pure and lovely must, by nature, also detest all that is impure and dirty. And that makes perfect sense.

God is not the only one who is unashamed to proclaim His wrath. The prophets in the Old Testament and the apostles in the New Testament were also unashamed to preach it.

Isaiah 30:27 – *See, the Name of the LORD comes from afar, with burning anger and dense clouds of smoke; his lips are full of wrath, and his tongue is a consuming fire.*

Romans 1:18 – *The wrath of God is being revealed from heaven against all the godlessness and wickedness of people, who suppress the truth by their wickedness.*

So, God is not ashamed to describe His wrath. The prophets and the apostles were not ashamed of it. And neither must we! By punishing evil, God exercises justice. He shows that He is a just God. The same is also true about hatred. We tend to see hate as a bad thing, but in truth, God hates things—many things. You can't love something without hating its opposite. So if you love the truth, you must hate the lie. If you don't hate the lie, then you don't really love the truth. If you love freedom, you must hate slavery. So if God loves us, He must hate that which would destroy us.

We praise human courts of law when they exercise justice against those who have committed evil acts. How much more should we praise a holy God who, in His wrath, executes *perfect* justice against evildoers? Scripture testifies that we will rejoice when God fully executes His wrath in the future against all His enemies—a concept that may be a little hard to grasp at present since we are still in the flesh.

> **Deuteronomy 32:43** – *Rejoice, you nations, with his people, for he will avenge the blood of his servants; he will take vengeance on his enemies and make atonement for his land and people.*

> **Revelation 19:1-3** – *After this I heard what sounded like the roar of a great multitude in heaven shouting: "Hallelujah! Salvation and glory and power belong to our God, for true and just are his judgments. He has condemned the great prostitute who corrupted the earth by her adulteries. He has avenged on her the blood of his servants." And again they shouted: "Hallelujah! The smoke from her goes up for ever and ever."*

We learn from these verses this truth: Just as we thank and praise God for showing His mercy and love, we should also thank and praise Him for displaying His wrath.

To the biblical writers, the gospel did not start with "God is love." It began with God being righteous and holy and that we all have fallen short of His holy standard. We are not right with God and so need to be right with Him. That was their starting point of gospel preaching, which should also be our starting point. Therefore, rather than being uneasy with the idea of the wrath of God, I hope we strive to unashamedly proclaim this attribute of God just as we do the other attributes.

What, then, are the implications of the truths concerning the wrath of God?

Four Implications for the Christian

1. We No Longer Have to Fear God's Wrath

Though we were (past tense) children of wrath (Ephesians 2:3), we are now children of God and co-heirs with Christ (Romans 8:16-17). We are promised in 1 Thessalonians 1:10b that "Jesus…rescues us from the coming wrath."

Unbelievers do not like the subject of God's wrath because, deep inside, they know they are guilty. Their only hope is in their self-righteousness and that their good works will get them into heaven. It is not a strong hope when one relies on one's own efforts. However, as believers, we are not relying on our righteousness. We rely on Christ's righteousness alone, which completely satisfies God's holy standards. That is why we have the solid and unshakeable hope that we are safe in Christ and thus no longer fear God's wrath.

2. We Will Thank God More

Knowing we will not experience God's wrath will cause us to thank God even more. When we realize our eternal future is very secure—not because of what we have done—but because of what God has done through Jesus for us, we will constantly abound in thanksgiving (Psalm 116:12-13).

3. We Will Fear God More and Thus Hate Sin More

While the genuine Christian will never experience God's wrath in the sense of losing salvation, a believer can sometimes expect severe discipline when there is unrepentant sin (1 Corinthians 11:28-32). Constant reflection of God's wrath enables the believer to take sin seriously, not make excuses for sinful living, and thus hate sin more. Living a life that fears the Lord in a practical sense means hating sin more, as Proverbs 8:13 declares, "To fear the LORD is to hate evil; I hate pride and arrogance, evil behavior and perverse speech."

4. We Will Urge People to Flee from the Wrath of God

John the Baptist urged the people to escape God's wrath by repenting of their sins (Matthew 3:7). Jesus spoke more about hell than anyone else and called us to fear God by turning to Him (Matthew 10:28). Paul warned the people to turn to Christ because he understood the wrath of God (2 Corinthians 5:11).

Preaching about hell is not an unloving act. On the contrary, it is a very loving thing—no matter what the world says! If we love someone, how can we not tell them about the eternal danger that awaits them if they continue living without Christ? The *key* is not only to preach on God's wrath but also to proclaim the forgiveness He offers through Christ's sacrifice on the cross (Psalm 130:3; Romans 3:25-26).

Two Implications for the Non-Christian

1. God's Past/Present Wrath Guarantees Future Wrath

In the Past. Adam and Eve's expulsion from the garden of Eden (Genesis 3), the destruction of everything on this earth, except those in Noah's Ark by the universal flood (Genesis 7:23), the destruction of Sodom and Gomorrah (Genesis 19), and the destruction of Jerusalem by Rome in A.D. 70 are just a few historically proven illustrations of God's wrath against those who rejected Him.

In the Present. John 3:36b says, "Whoever rejects the Son will not see life, for God's wrath remains on them." Those far away from Jesus are currently under God's wrath. Romans 1:18 says, "The wrath of God is being revealed from heaven against all the godlessness and wickedness of people, who suppress the truth by their wickedness." In the present, this wrath is displayed through God abandoning sinners to their own ways so they can reap the consequences as they persist in wickedness (Romans 1:24-32).

In the Future. We read in 2 Thessalonians 1:7b-9, "This will happen when the Lord Jesus is revealed from heaven in blazing fire with his powerful angels. He will punish those who do not know God and do not obey the gospel of our Lord Jesus. They will be punished with everlasting destruction and shut out from the presence of the Lord and from the glory of his might." Revelation 6-20 describes in greater detail God's future and final wrath that is to be poured out on those who refuse to obey the gospel of the Lord Jesus Christ.

The Bible teaches that God cannot lie (Titus 1:2, NASB). Since He has promised to judge all those who reject Christ, He will keep His word. Just because God is not immediately judging every act of evil, one must not be deceived into thinking that He will *never* judge sin (Ecclesiastes 8:11-14).

There is a story of an ungodly farmer who lived in a community of godly farmers. When the godly farmers met in a country church every Sunday morning, this man would run his tractor to cause a disturbance. He did this for many months. Finally, when harvest time came in October, his land had the highest yield per acre

Attribute 8: The Wrath of God

in that community. With pride, he wrote to the local newspaper about how Christians could explain his success when he did this against God and His people.

The pastor responded with one sentence: *"God does not settle all his accounts in October."*

Dear friend, if you are not a Christian, don't think God must be pleased with you because all is well today. Don't mistake His patience as Him being okay with your sin. His goodness is not to be abused but is designed to lead you to true repentance and faith in His Son (Romans 2:4-5).

2. God's Future Wrath Should Make You Run to Jesus

The Bible says, "It is a terrifying thing to fall into the hands of the living God" (Hebrews 10:31). Please realize that your sins have made you an enemy of God. As a result, His wrath rests on you in the present and awaits you in the future. Please cry out for mercy. You must desire to "flee from the coming wrath" (Matthew 3:7) and run to the cross where Jesus Christ took God's wrath upon Himself so that He can freely pardon your sins. You need to throw away all self-confidence and humbly cry out, "God, be merciful to me, the sinner!" (Luke 18:13, NASB). That's the only way you can be delivered from the coming wrath.

Dear friend, nothing is as sweet as the goodness and patience of God. However, nothing is also more terrible than His coming wrath. The same water that can quench your thirst can also be your terrible enemy when it comes as a flood. The same fire that can cook your food can also be your terrible enemy when it burns you. Likewise, the same God who is patient and good to you today will one day turn against you in terrible vengeance. None can deliver you from His hand on that day. No amount of crying or pleading will save you. Look to Jesus, who died on the cross for sins and was raised to prove that His sacrifice was accepted as full payment for sins. Through Jesus, there is complete forgiveness.

So, turn to Him in true repentance and faith—right now while there is still time! He will accept you no matter how bad you have been and give you a new beginning! Do not die in your sins. Please receive God's free gift of eternal life through Jesus Christ (Romans 6:23)!

Discussion Questions

1. How has this chapter affected your view of God's wrath?

2. What life changes could you make in light of this attribute of God?

3. How does this attribute of God affect your prayers?

4. How does this attribute of God affect your evangelism?

Attribute 8: The Wrath of God

SCRIPTURE VERSE FOR MEDITATION/MEMORIZATION

Psalm 7:11 – *God is a righteous judge, a God who displays his wrath every day.*

PRAYER

Father, Often I'm prone to forgetting that even though You are my Heavenly Father, You are also a God of wrath. You hate sin and will judge it. I'm grateful that the Lord Jesus absorbed all the wrath that I deserve. Please make me walk with fear and trembling that will protect me from taking sin lightly. May Your wrath against all who rebel against You cause me to plead with the lost ones around me to flee to Jesus, who alone can rescue us from Your coming judgment. Protect me from shying away from talking about Your wrath when presenting the gospel to people, but to preach it in love and with a sense of great seriousness. Amen!

HYMNS/SONGS

1. "Day of Judgment! Day of Wonders" by John Newton
2. "Sinner, Art Thou Still Secure?" by John Newton
3. "Divine Wrath" by John Keble
4. "In Mercy, Not in Wrath" by John Newton

ATTRIBUTE 9

The Faithfulness of God

The faithfulness of God means He can be trusted to fulfill all His promises.

Solomon wrote in Proverbs 20:6, "Many claim to have unfailing love, but a faithful person who can find?" We live in a world that proves the truthfulness of this proverb. Friendships, marriages, and business dealings fall apart because of the unfaithfulness of human beings. Perhaps you, too, have felt the deep pain of betrayal—from the very same individuals who promised to be faithful to the very end.

In the darkness of such realities, this attribute of God—His faithfulness—brings great comfort to the hurting soul. The Bible declares God's faithfulness very early in Deuteronomy 7:9, "Know therefore that the LORD your God is God; he is the faithful God, keeping his covenant of love to a thousand generations of those who love him and keep his commandments." We read later in Deuteronomy 32:4, "He is the Rock, his works are perfect, and all his ways are just. A faithful God who does no wrong, upright and just is he."

Unlike fallen human beings whose faithfulness often wavers, God never wavers in His faithfulness. Moses reminded us in Numbers 23:19, "God is not human, that he should lie, not a human being, that he should change his mind. Does he speak and then not act? Does he promise and not fulfill?" The psalmist Ethan the Ezrahite wrote in Psalm 89:8, "Who is like you, LORD God Almighty? You, LORD, are mighty, and your faithfulness surrounds you." Paul reminded us in Titus 1:2 (NASB) that "God cannot lie." The writer of Hebrews said, "It is impossible for God to lie" (Hebrews 6:18). Agur reminded us that "every word of God is flawless" (Proverbs 30:5). All these verses teach us that God can be entirely relied upon to keep His promises. He will never prove unfaithful to those who trust Him wholeheartedly (Psalm 34:22).

Wayne Grudem rightly stated: "Essence of true faith is taking God at his word and relying on him to do what he has promised."[23] And because God is faithful to fulfill all His promises, the believer can confidently say that because of the LORD's great love, we are not consumed, for His compassions never fail. They are new every morning; great is His faithfulness. And we can also say to ourselves, "The LORD is my portion; therefore I will wait for Him" (Lamentations 3:22-24).

---

[23] *Systematic Theology*, p. 195

Attribute 9: The Faithfulness of God

The Bible is filled with illustrations of God's faithfulness in that He fulfills His promises. Let's look at a few examples.

1. God promised Noah, as recorded in Genesis 8:22, "As long as the earth endures, seedtime and harvest, cold and heat, summer and winter, day and night will never cease." Year after year, we see this being fulfilled.

2. In Genesis 15:13-16, God predicted to Abraham the 400-year slavery that the Jews would undergo with a promise of His deliverance. Exodus 12:41 records the fulfillment of this deliverance: "At the end of the 430 years, to the very day, all the LORD's divisions left Egypt."

3. In Isaiah 7:14, we are given the prophecy concerning the virgin birth of Jesus Christ, "Therefore the LORD himself will give you a sign: The virgin will conceive and give birth to a son, and will call him Immanuel." Matthew 1:22-25 records the fulfillment of this prophecy.

More examples could be cited in addition to the three mentioned above. But the point is clear as Hebrews 10:23 states, "He who promised is faithful." And the remainder of this chapter will focus on the 2 aspects of God's faithfulness:

1. In the lives of His children
2. In the lives of His enemies.

1. God's Faithfulness: In the Lives of His Children

In Preserving Them. We are told in 1 Corinthians 1:8-9, "He will also keep you firm to the end so that you will be blameless on the day of our Lord Jesus Christ. God is faithful, who has called you into fellowship with his Son, Jesus Christ our Lord." In the ultimate sense, the preservation of our salvation is grounded upon the faithfulness of God. Jesus spoke these precious words concerning the security of our salvation, "My sheep listen to my voice; I know them, and they follow me. I give them eternal life, and they shall never perish; no one will snatch them out of my hand" (John 10:27-28). Besides, Jesus also prayed for our preservation in His high priestly prayer: "Holy Father, protect them by the power of your name, the name you gave me, so that they may be one as we are one" (John 17:11).

In Disciplining Them. Not only is God's faithfulness displayed in preserving us, but it's also displayed in Him disciplining us. Hebrews 12:4-11 is a passage that encourages us to endure as we go through God's disciplining process. The writer says that being disciplined (or trained) by God is proof positive that we *are* His true children, and a faithful God does it in order to make us resemble more His Son. Here are portions of this passage that highlight this truth:

> **Hebrews 12: 7-8, 10b-11** – *Endure hardship as discipline; God is treating you as his children. For what children are not disciplined by their*

Attribute 9: The Faithfulness of God

father? If you are not disciplined—and everyone undergoes discipline—then you are not legitimate, not true sons and daughters at all...God disciplines us for our good, in order that we may share in his holiness. No discipline seems pleasant at the time, but painful. Later on, however, it produces a harvest of righteousness and peace for those who have been trained by it.

No wonder the psalmist said, when being disciplined, these words, "I know, LORD, that your laws are righteous, and that in faithfulness you have afflicted me" (Psalm 119:75). A faithful God does what is necessary, even though it may be painful, to make us more holy.

In Glorifying Them. Not only is God's faithfulness displayed in preserving us and in disciplining us, but His faithfulness will also be displayed in our ultimate glorification, where we will be made like Jesus. We are promised in Romans 8:30, "And those he predestined, he also called; those he called, he also justified; those he justified, he also glorified." Notice that the phrase "he also glorified" appears in the past tense even though it is yet to happen. What's the point, you may ask? Simple. In God's sight, our glorification is a done deal. That's why it's in the past tense. That's how much we can trust a faithful God to keep His promises. No wonder Paul wrote in Philippians 1:6 that he was "confident...that he who began a good work...will carry it on to completion until the day of Christ Jesus."

All our promises of glorification are grounded in the faithfulness of God as stated in 1 Thessalonians 5:23-24, "May God himself, the God of peace, sanctify you through and through. May your whole spirit, soul and body be kept blameless at the coming of our Lord Jesus Christ. The one who calls you is faithful, and he will do it." God's faithfulness to glorify Paul led him to say, even in the midst of his great sufferings, these confident words, "That is why I am suffering as I am. Yet this is no cause for shame, because I know whom I have believed, and am convinced that he is able to guard what I have entrusted to him until that day" (2 Timothy 1:12).

So, in light of these three areas—preserving, disciplining, and finally glorifying us—we see God's faithfulness displayed toward us, His children. These truths should cause us to trust God even in dark moments and never grumble or give up. We are to keep persevering in faith and to be free from anxiety. That's what the faithful men and women of the faith described in Hebrews 11 did. And they were not disappointed. We won't be disappointed in the end either because God is faithful to keep ALL His promises to us.

We don't have to give up even when battling sin and going through severe temptations. We are told in 1 Corinthians 10:13, "No temptation has overtaken you except what is common to mankind. And God is faithful; he will not let you be tempted beyond what you

Attribute 9: The Faithfulness of God

can bear. But when you are tempted, he will also provide a way out so that you can endure it." When Paul said that God will "provide a way out," he did not mean that we will necessarily *escape* trials. Instead, he meant we can trust this faithful God to give us the strength to *endure* the trials—even when it may seem overwhelming—and not succumb to temptation as long as we keep trusting Him. Sometimes, even if it means death is the outcome, God is still faithful to strengthen us so that we will never disown Him to the very end!

Let's not forget this faithful God has also promised us: "Never will I leave you; never will I forsake you" (Hebrews 13:5). Jesus has promised to be with us to the very end, "And surely I am with you always, to the very end of the age" (Matthew 28:20). Trust is taking God at His word and relying on Him to do what He has promised because He is a faithful God who will keep all His promises—even when the situation looks bleak. The Old Testament prophet, Habakkuk, did that very thing and, as a result, experienced joy in his heart: "Though the fig tree does not bud and there are no grapes on the vines, though the olive crop fails and the fields produce no food, though there are no sheep in the pen and no cattle in the stalls, yet I will rejoice in the LORD, I will be joyful in God my Savior" (Habakkuk 3:17-18).

Dear Christian, are you going through a tough time? Are you finding it very hard to get through just another day? Don't give up. Even if things seem hopeless, like Habakkuk, trust this faithful God. He *will* carry you till the end. Press on in faith without giving up! He has promised in Isaiah 46:4, "Even to your old age and gray hairs I am he, I am he who will sustain you. I have made you and I will carry you; I will sustain you and I will rescue you."

2. God's Faithfulness: In the Lives of His Enemies

Just as God is faithful to keep His promises to His children, He is *equally* faithful to keep His promises to judge those who reject Him and thus remain His enemies. In other words, He is faithful, both as Savior and Judge. Past judgments of God, without a doubt, prove His faithfulness in judging those who rebel against Him. He judged the world that did not repent during Noah's time through the worldwide flood that destroyed them all (Genesis 6-8). Not one person survived except Noah and his family, the only ones to have found grace in God's sight. And God, likewise, also judged the unbelievers during the wilderness journey because they failed to trust Him to bring them to the promised land (Numbers 14:26-34; Hebrews 3:15-19). Since God displayed His faithfulness in keeping His word of judgment in the past, we can be sure He will be faithful to do the same in the future as well!

God has promised a future judgment of fire in the lake of fire or hell for all who fail to turn from their sins and put their trust in Jesus Christ. Revelation 20:15 says,

Attribute 9: The Faithfulness of God

"Anyone whose name was not found written in the book of life was thrown into the lake of fire." And this will happen "when the Lord Jesus is revealed from heaven in blazing fire with his powerful angels. He will punish those who do not know God and do not obey the gospel of our Lord Jesus. They will be punished with everlasting destruction and shut out from the presence of the Lord and from the glory of his might" (2 Thessalonians 1:7b-9).

In light of God's faithfulness in keeping His judgment promises, what should be your response if you are not His child and thus His enemy?

First, ask God to open your eyes to see that you have sinned against Him, your Creator. Then acknowledge to Him that you have sinned and are guilty of punishment. Don't give any excuses. Just an explicit acknowledgment, "I have sinned against You. I'm guilty, Lord." Tell Him you are sorry for your sins and want to turn from a sinful lifestyle. That's what the Bible calls "repentance." But that's not enough. Finally, by faith, you need to accept the forgiveness God offers through Jesus Christ, believing that Jesus paid the full price for sins by living a perfect life, dying on the cross, and rising again. That's how you can be saved from your sins and from God's wrath. And that's also how you become His child (John 1:12).

The Bible promises that "Everyone who calls on the name of the Lord will be saved" (Romans 10:13). Call out to Him. Embrace Jesus as your Lord and Savior.

Follow your repentance and faith by *publicly* testifying in the waters of baptism by immersion (Acts 8:36-38). Baptism is the first step of obedience *after* becoming a child of God (Acts 2:41).

Jesus invites all who are burdened by their sins and guilt to come to Him: "Come to me, all you who are weary and burdened, and I will give you rest" (Matthew 11:28). And for those willing to come, He gives this promise: whoever comes to Me I will never drive away (John 6:37b). Jesus is faithful to keep His promises. He can be trusted. Come and experience His forgiveness. Don't let anything or anyone stop you from coming to Christ. *The cost of staying away from Jesus is far higher than the cost of coming to Jesus.* It's okay if you must give up everything—even your life—if that gets you united with Jesus. In the end, you will find Jesus—the real and lasting treasure as being more than worthy than all that you gave up.

Please understand, friend, that this faithful God is also a *forgiving* God. Have your sins washed away by the blood of His Son Jesus. I appeal to you with a sincere heart. Come to Jesus. Meet Him as a Savior rather than as a Judge. Flee from the judgment to come. No matter how much you have sinned and messed up, you can find true peace and rest in Jesus. And then, after you come to Jesus, you also, along with the other children of God, can say like David, "Your love, LORD, reaches to the heavens, your faithfulness to the skies" (Psalm 36:5).

Discussion Questions

1. How has this chapter affected your view of God's faithfulness?
2. What life changes could you make in light of this attribute of God?
3. How does this attribute of God affect your prayers?
4. How does this attribute of God affect your evangelism?

Scripture Verse for Meditation/Memorization

Psalm 89:8 – *Who is like you, Lord God Almighty? You, Lord, are mighty, and your faithfulness surrounds you.*

Prayer

Gracious God and loving Father, in a world where people so casually break their promises, I praise You for being a God who is faithful to keep all His promises. Even when I am walking through a dark valley, help me to remember Your faithfulness. You have promised to be with me at all times. By faith, help me take You at Your word, even when You feel absent. Strengthen my heart to trust that You who began a good work in me will complete it someday. And move my heart to imitate You in keeping my promises to others. Please help me to be marked by faithfulness. Amen!

Hymns/Songs

1. "Great Is Thy Faithfulness" by Thomas O. Chisolm
2. "What a Faithful God" by Robert & Dawn Critchley
3. "Faithful One So Unchanging" by Brian Doersken
4. "The Steadfast Love of the Lord" by Robert Davidson

ATTRIBUTE 10

The Sovereignty of God

The sovereignty of God refers to His complete control over all the events of life, including reasons known to Himself those acts that are in defiance of His revealed will as found in Scripture.

The following story is a great illustration of how a Christian should think when it comes to the sovereignty of God:

> *In the year 1902, a young English boy came down to breakfast to find his father reading the newspaper which carried news of preparations for the first coronation in Britain in 64 years. In the middle of breakfast, the father turned to his wife and said, "Oh, I am sorry to see this worded like that."*
>
> *She said, "What is it?"*
>
> *"Why," he replied, "here is a proclamation that on a certain date Prince Edward will be crowned*

king at Westminster, and there is no Deo volente, God willing."

The words stuck in the young boy's mind for the very reason that, on the appointed date, the future Edward VII was ill with appendicitis, and the coronation had to be postponed. At this time, at the end of Queen Victoria's reign, the political, economic, and military power of the British Empire was at its zenith.

Yet, for all its great might, Great Britain could not carry out its planned coronation on the appointed date. Was the omission of "God willing" from the proclamation and the subsequent postponement of the coronation merely a coincidence, two events without any relation to one another? Or did God cause Prince Edward to have appendicitis to show that He was "in control"?

We don't know why the situation occurred as it did. One thing we do know, however: whether we acknowledge it with Deo volente or not, we cannot carry out any plan apart from God's will. The Bible leaves no doubt about that fact...God is in control; He is sovereign. He does whatever pleases him and determines whether we can do what we have planned. This is the essence of God's sovereignty; his absolute independence to do as he pleases and his absolute control over the actions of all his creations. No creature, person, or empire can either thwart his will or act outside the bounds of his will.[24]

Arthur Pink rightly said: "When we say that God is sovereign we affirm His right to govern the universe, which He has made for His own glory, just as He pleases. We affirm that *His right* is the right of the Potter over the clay...We affirm that He is under no rule or law outside of His own will and nature, *that God is a law unto Himself,* and that He is under no obligation to give an account of His matters to any."[25] Yes, God is indeed in complete control over all events of life, including reasons known only to Himself and of those acts that are in defiance of His revealed will. In His great wisdom, He uses even the evil actions of humans and of the devil to accomplish His good purposes.

Here are a few Scriptures that teach us about God's sovereignty.

> **Genesis 50:20** – *You intended to harm me, but God intended it for good to accomplish what is now being done, the saving of many lives.*

> **Isaiah 46:9-10** – *Remember the former things, those of long ago; I am God, and there is no other; I am God, and there is none like me. I make known the end from the beginning, from ancient*

---

[24] Jerry Bridges, *Trusting God: Even When Life Hurts*, (pp. 35-36) Navpress. Kindle Edition.
[25] *The Sovereignty of God*, (Monee: IL, 2023) p. 18.

times, what is still to come. I say, 'My purpose will stand, and I will do all that I please.

Job 42:2 – *I know that you can do all things; no purpose of yours can be thwarted.*

Psalm 115:3 – *Our God is in heaven; he does whatever pleases him.*

Proverbs 19:21 – *Many are the plans in a person's heart, but it is the LORD's purpose that prevails.*

Proverbs 21:30 – *There is no wisdom, no insight, no plan that can succeed against the LORD.*

Lamentations 3:37 – *Who can speak and have it happen if the LORD has not decreed it?*

Paul told us that God "works out everything in conformity with the purpose of his will" (Ephesians 1:11). That's sovereignty in a nutshell: God working out everything according to His will and pleasure. God is *never* the author of sin (Habakkuk 1:13; James 1:13). Yet, in keeping with His sovereignty, He uses even the evil that happens to ultimately accomplish His good and glorious purposes (Genesis 50:20) without ever compromising His holy nature. How He is able to do this is a mystery that our finite minds can never fully comprehend.

Here are Scriptures supporting the truth that God is always in control even when evil happens.

Exodus 4:11 – *The* LORD *said to him (Moses), "Who gave human beings their mouths? Who makes them deaf or mute? Who gives them sight or makes them blind? Is it not I, the* LORD*?"*

Deuteronomy 32:39 – *See now that I myself am he! There is no god besides me. I put to death and I bring to life, I have wounded and I will heal, and no one can deliver out of my hand.*

Job 2:10 – *You are talking like a foolish woman. Shall we accept good from God, and not trouble?" In all this, Job did not sin in what he said.*[26]

Isaiah 45:7 – *I form the light and create darkness, I bring prosperity and create disaster; I, the* LORD*, do all these things.*

Lamentations 3:37-38 – *Who can speak and have it happen if the* LORD *has not decreed it? Is it not from the mouth of the Most High that both calamities and good things come?*

It's also interesting to note that Elisha, whom God used to heal others,[27] died of a disease.

2 Kings 13:14 – *Now Elisha had been suffering from the illness from which he died. Jehoash king of Israel went down to see him and wept over him. "My father! My father!" he cried. "The chariots and horsemen of Israel!"*

---

[26] Job's response to his wife who told to curse God and die (Job 2:9).
[27] E.g., Shunammite's son in 2 Kings 4:18-37, and Naaman in 2 Kings 5.

So, we can see clearly from the above Scriptures that God is sovereign over all affairs—both good and evil.

What, then, are some practical implications of God's sovereignty? A total of four are listed below.

1. It Honors God as the Supreme Being in the Universe

In other words, this attribute acknowledges God to be God! It acknowledges His right to rule as King over everything. It reminds us that He is the Creator and we are the created ones. God does not need us. On the other hand, we need Him for the very next breath!

Through the prophet Isaiah, God tells us, "I am the LORD; that is my name! I will not yield my glory to another or my praise to idols" (Isaiah 42:8). By acknowledging God's absolute sovereignty, we give Him full glory. After all, we are created for God's glory: "Everyone who is called by my name, whom I created for my glory, whom I formed and made" (Isaiah 43:7)! So, let's give God His rightful place as the Supreme Being in the universe by acknowledging His sovereignty over all things!

2. It Humbles Us

Since God is always after a humble heart, what could be more humbling than the constant acknowledgment that "God is in charge of everything, and we are not!"

Attribute 10: The Sovereignty of God

This truth exalts God for who He is and what He has done for us!

Nebuchadnezzar, one of the most powerful kings who ever ruled the world, learned the hard way how a sovereign God humbles man's pride. His pride had deceived his heart as he boasted of his achievements and failed to give glory to God: "Is not this the great Babylon I have built as the royal residence, by my mighty power and for the glory of my majesty?" (Daniel 4:30). Notice how God cut him down in judgment by reminding him that He and not a mere human is the One who is sovereign over all things. "Even as the words were on his lips, a voice came from heaven, 'This is what is decreed for you, King Nebuchadnezzar: Your royal authority has been taken from you. You will be driven away from people and will live with the wild animals; you will eat grass like the ox. Seven times will pass by for you until you acknowledge that the Most High is sovereign over all kingdoms on earth and gives them to anyone he wishes'" (Daniel 4:31-32).

Having been humbled, Nebuchadnezzar finally acknowledged that God is sovereign over all: "At the end of that time, I, Nebuchadnezzar, raised my eyes toward heaven, and my sanity was restored. Then I praised the Most High; I honored and glorified him who lives forever. His dominion is an eternal dominion; his kingdom endures from generation to generation. All the peoples of the earth are regarded as nothing. He does as he pleases with the powers of heaven and the peoples of the earth. No one can hold back his hand or say to him: 'What have you done?'… Now I, Nebuchadnezzar, praise and exalt and glorify the King of heaven, because everything he does is right and all his ways are just. And those who walk in pride he is able to humble" (Daniel 4:34-35, 37).

The more we embrace this doctrine of God's sovereignty, the more we will grow in humility.

3. It Brings Great Comfort During Times of Intense Trial

The sovereign Lord of the universe, who controls everything, has chosen to show us His love and mercy. What did we ever do to deserve such love? Nothing! And if God loves us despite our great sins and has made us His children, why should we be conquered by fear when going through trials—even when those trials are intense?

Joseph had great confidence in God's sovereignty. That is why, despite having gone through extremely difficult times, he could still say to his brothers these words: "You intended to harm me, but God intended it for good to accomplish what is now being done, the saving of many lives" (Genesis 50:20). He knew God controlled all circumstances of his life and hence did not cave into despair even when things got terrible for him.

Attribute 10: The Sovereignty of God

Jerry Bridges wrote:

> God is in control, but in His control He allows us to experience pain. The pain is very real. We hurt, we suffer. But in the midst of our suffering, we must believe that God is in control; he is still sovereign. As author Margaret Clarkson has so beautifully written, "The sovereignty of God is the one impregnable rock to which the suffering human heart must cling. The circumstances surrounding our lives are no accident: they may be the work of evil, but that evil is held firmly within the mighty hand of our sovereign God...All evil is subject to Him, and evil cannot touch His children unless He permits it. God is the Lord of human history and of the personal history of every member of His redeemed family.
>
> Not only are the willful malevolent acts of other people under God's sovereign control, so also are the mistakes and failures of other people. Did another driver go through a red light, strike your car, and send you to the hospital with multiple fractures? Did a physician fail to detect your cancer in its early stages, when it would have been treatable? Did you end up with an incompetent instructor in a very important course in college or an inept supervisor that blocked your career in business? All of these circumstances are under the controlling hand of our sovereign God,

who is working them out in our lives for our good.[28]

Belief in the sovereignty of God should include the thought that even *this* particular trial I am undergoing right now had to pass through the nail-pierced hands of a sovereign and loving Christ who is in total control. He will accomplish all His purposes through this trial. This knowledge brings great comfort, especially when things around us keep falling apart! We are always safe in the arms of a loving God who controls all things. Let us remember that even in the midst of dark times.

4. It Does Not Cancel Out Human Responsibility

The sovereignty of God does not contradict or cancel out the freedom or responsibility of human beings—even though our finite minds may not be able to comprehend this fact entirely. Human actions do not limit God, nor are His purposes thwarted by our efforts. God's sovereignty includes all our actions—except that God is never responsible for our sins. A good example is found in Acts 2:23, "This man [referring to Jesus] was handed over to you by God's deliberate plan and foreknowledge [Divine Sovereignty]; and you, with the help of wicked men, put him to death by nailing him to the cross [Human Responsibility]." God held to account the people responsible for the death of His Son.

---

[28] *Trusting God*, pp. 39-40.

Yet, Jesus going to the cross was part of His sovereign plan!

The bottom line is this: Divine sovereignty does not cancel out human responsibility, nor does human responsibility cancel out divine sovereignty. Both these doctrines are taught in the Scriptures. Our finite minds cannot reconcile these truths. Yet, they are perfectly reconciled in the eyes of a sovereign, infinite, and all-wise God whose ways are beyond our understanding.

So, those are four implications to think about as we marvel and submit to this attribute of God being sovereign over all things.

If you are a child of God, rejoice and rest because you are in the hands of a God who controls every event in your life. No matter what happens, you will soon be with Him for all eternity. Until then, submit to His rule over you. Pursue a life that focuses on glorifying Him at all times—both good and bad.

If you are not God's child yet, please understand that you cannot fight against this sovereign God and win. He has commanded you to turn from your sins and put your trust in His Son, Jesus Christ, who paid the price for sins. Only then can you be forgiven of your sins, become His child, and escape from the coming judgment. So, please do it today. Experience the peace and joy that comes from having your sins washed away by the blood of Jesus. Do not delay!

Discussion Questions

1. How has this chapter affected your view of God's sovereignty?
2. What life changes could you make in light of this attribute of God?
3. How does this attribute of God affect your prayers?
4. How does this attribute of God affect your evangelism?

Scripture Verse for Meditation/Memorization

Psalm 115:3 – *Our God is in heaven; he does whatever pleases him.*

Prayer

O LORD,

I hang on Thee; I see, believe, live, when thy will, not mine, is done;

I can plead nothing in myself in regard to any worthiness and grace, in regard of thy providence and promises, but only thy good pleasure. If thy mercy make me poor and vile, blessed be thou!

Prayers arising from my needs are preparations for future mercies; Help me to honor thee by believing before I feel, for great is the sin if I make feeling a cause of faith...

Help me to pray in faith and so find thy will, by leaning hard on thy rich mercy, by believing thou wilt give what thou hast promised;

Strengthen me to pray with conviction that whatever I receive in thy git, so that I may pray until prayer be granted...

So shall I wait thy will, pray for it to be done, and by thy grace become fully obedient.[29]

Amen!

Hymns/Songs

1. "Our Sovereign God" by Tom Pennington
2. "Lord, the King of Kings Art Thou" by Witness Lee
3. "Sovereign Ruler of the Skies" by John Ryland
4. "Whatever My God Ordains Is Right" by Samuel Rodigast

---

[29] Arthur Bennet, *Valley of Vision*, pp. 14-15.

Attribute 11

The Patience of God

The patience of God refers to His ability to withhold His judgment, even for an extended period.[30]

God revealed Himself to Moses, He proclaimed His attributes in this way, "The LORD, the LORD, the compassionate and gracious God, slow to anger, abounding in love and faithfulness" (Exodus 34:6b). Did you notice that phrase, "slow to anger"? God is so patient that He does not punish people immediately but often withholds His judgment, even for an extended period.

Arthur Pink quotes Stephen Charnock's words on God's patience in this manner:

---

[30] While God's patience can be seen as a specific attribute of His, as in this chapter, one can also view His patience as a *result* of His other attributes, such as compassion and mercy. That's why we often find in the Bible God's patience appearing alongside or following the terms that describe His compassionate, gracious, and merciful nature. See various Scriptures listed in this chapter that attest to this truth.

It is a part of the Divine goodness and mercy, yet differs from both. God being the greatest goodness, hath the greatest mildness; mildness is always the companion of true goodness, and the greater the goodness, the greater the mildness. Who so holy as Christ, and who so meek? God's slowness to anger is a branch of His mercy: "the Lord is full of compassion, slow to anger" (Psalm 145:8).[31]

Here are a few references to God's patience in the Old Testament:

> **Numbers 14:18** – *The* LORD *is slow to anger, abounding in love and forgiving sin and rebellion.*
>
> **Psalm 86:15** – *But you,* LORD, *are a compassionate and gracious God, slow to anger, abounding in love and faithfulness.*
>
> **Psalm 103:8** – *The* LORD *is compassionate and gracious, slow to anger, abounding in love.*
>
> **Psalm 145:8** – *The* LORD *is gracious and compassionate, slow to anger and rich in love.*

While explaining why he ran away from God's command to preach to the Ninevites, Jonah highlights God's patience as the reason for his disobedience. "He prayed to the LORD, 'Isn't this what I said, LORD, when I was still at home? That is what I tried to forestall by

---

[31] *Attributes of God*, p. 79.

fleeing to Tarshish. I knew that you are a gracious and compassionate God, *slow to anger* and abounding in love, a God who relents from sending calamity'" (Jonah 4:2, emphasis mine). In other words, Jonah, a prophet, knew about God's patience and that He would forgive even the wicked Ninevites if they repented. He did not want them to be forgiven. So, he refused to preach the gospel to them—until God *made* him obey His command! This clearly shows that God's patience, coupled with His love for sinners, caused Him to forgive even the wicked Ninevites. The prophet Nahum also, while preaching to the Ninevites many years later, wrote about God's patience as He called them to repentance, "The LORD is slow to anger but great in power; the Lord will not leave the guilty unpunished" (Nahum 1:3)!

To those who say the God of the Old Testament is *only* a punishing God and rarely shows love, these verses mentioned above stand as a rebuke. What patience God showed to people who sinned over long periods!

When we come to the New Testament, we find several references highlighting God's patience. Below are a few:

> **Romans 2:4** – *Or do you show contempt for the riches of his kindness, forbearance and patience, not realizing that God's kindness is intended to lead you to repentance?*

1 Timothy 1:16 – *But for that very reason I was shown mercy so that in me, the worst of sinners, Christ Jesus might display his immense patience as an example for those who would believe in him and receive eternal life.*

Paul, after stating, "Christ Jesus came into the world to save sinners—of whom I am the worst" (1 Timothy 1:15), went on to say that even though he was the worst of sinners, "for that very reason I was shown mercy." Why? This way, Jesus could "display his immense patience as an example for those who would believe in him and receive eternal life." In other words, if God was so patient with Paul, who fought so much against Jesus and still saved him, will He not also save other sinners—if they accept His offer of eternal life by placing their faith in His Son, Jesus?

Peter also refers to God's patience in the past when the ark was being built: "God waited patiently in the days of Noah while the ark was being built. In it only a few people, eight in all, were saved through water" (1 Peter 3:20). In His immense patience, God waited over 100 years for people to repent, thus avoiding His judgment. He could have killed them all right away for their wickedness. Yet, His patience caused him to hold back the judgment for a very long time—even though He knew they would not repent (Genesis 6:13, 18).

Paul says something very similar in Romans 9:22, "God, although choosing to show his wrath and make his power known, bore with great patience the objects of his wrath—prepared for destruction." He is patient even with people who will ultimately face His wrath and destruction for failing to turn to Him in repentance. It is incredible when we pause and think about God's patience toward those who will still reject Him in the final analysis!

So, what, then, are the implications of this attribute of God in our lives?

FOR THE CHRISTIAN

We are to exhibit patience in our relationships with one another. That is the main implication. Often, we are so quick to get angry with people. Such an attitude sometimes leads to retaliation in hurtful ways because we feel hurt. Yet, the Bible repeatedly calls us to pursue patience (being slow to get angry) in our relationships with each another.

Proverbs 19:11 – *A person's wisdom yields patience; it is to one's glory to overlook an offense.*

1 Corinthians 13:4 – *Love is patient, love is kind. It does not envy, it does not boast, it is not proud.*

Colossians 3:12 – *Therefore, as God's chosen people, holy and dearly loved, clothe yourselves with compassion, kindness, humility, gentleness and patience.*

Ephesians 4:2 – *Be completely humble and gentle; be patient, bearing with one another in love.*

1 Thessalonians 5:14 – *And we urge you, brothers and sisters, warn those who are idle and disruptive, encourage the disheartened, help the weak, be patient with everyone.*

Peter reminds believers of God's patience toward His own as He waits for them to repent through these words: "The Lord is not slow in keeping his promise, as some understand slowness. Instead, he is patient with you, not wanting anyone to perish, but everyone to come to repentance" (2 Peter 3:9).

By constantly reflecting on how patient God *was* with us before we came to Him and *is* still patient with us—who fail Him so often *after* becoming His children, we too can develop a spirit of patience when dealing with people—even the most difficult ones when they sin against us! We don't need to seek revenge even when we are repeatedly insulted or overlooked. As Solomon wisely advised, "It is to one's glory to overlook an offense" (Proverbs 19:11b)! Chrysostom, a church leader from the past, said, "A patient man is one who, having the resources and opportunity to avenge himself, chooses to refrain from the exercise of these."

No one treated Lincoln with more contempt than Edwin Stanton, who denounced Lincoln's policies and called him a "low cunning clown." Stanton had nicknamed him "the original gorilla." He said that the

Attribute 11: The Patience of God

explorer Paul Du Chaillu was a fool to wander about in Africa trying to capture a gorilla when he could have found one easily in Springfield, Illinois. Lincoln said nothing in reply. In fact, he made Stanton his war minister because Stanton was the best man for the job. He treated him with every courtesy. The years wore on.

The night came when an assassin's bullet struck down Lincoln in a theatre. In a room off to the side where Lincoln's body was taken stood Stanton that night. As he looked down on the silent, rugged face of the President, Stanton said through his tears, "There lies the greatest ruler of men the world has ever seen."

The patience of love had conquered in the end as Romans 12:21 reminds us: "Do not be overcome by evil, but overcome evil with good." God is so patient even with the wicked who continually mock Him. Should we not imitate Him by being patient with those who hurt us? Like Father, like children! That's the goal!

How can we develop patience? It is important to remember that we cannot produce this patience on our own. We *need* the Holy Spirit to work this attribute of patience in our lives. One of the characteristics of the "fruit of the Spirit is...forbearance [patience]" (Galatians 5:22-23). When we make it a practice to submit to the Holy Spirit (which is living a life of obedience to the Scriptures), He (the Holy Spirit) produces the fruit of patience in us. That's the path to developing and displaying a spirit of patience in our relationships with each other.

For the Non-Christian

God's patience in dealing with sinners is seen in His waiting for nearly a century for people to repent. He gave them multiple opportunities to repent as He used Noah, "a preacher of righteousness" (2 Peter 2:5), to repeatedly call them to turn from their sins and turn to Him in faith. Yet, when they failed to repent, God *did* judge them.

In the same way, as God displays His patience toward you, His intention is for you to repent, as Paul reminds us in Romans 2:4, "Or do you show contempt for the riches of his kindness, forbearance and patience, not realizing that God's kindness is intended to lead you to repentance?" But if you fail to repent, there is a warning as seen in the next two verses: "But because of your stubbornness and your unrepentant heart, you are storing up wrath against yourself for the day of God's wrath, when his righteous judgment will be revealed. God will repay each person according to what they have done" (Romans 2:5-6).

The Old Testament issues the same warning also. Just because you are not judged today shouldn't deceive you into thinking you will *never* be judged in the future. Here is God's warning from Ecclesiastes 8:11-13, "When the sentence for a crime is not quickly carried out, people's hearts are filled with schemes to do wrong. Although a wicked person who commits a hundred crimes may live a long time, I know that it

Attribute 11: The Patience of God

will go better with those who fear God, who are reverent before him. Yet because the wicked do not fear God, it will not go well with them, and their days will not lengthen like a shadow." Just because all is well today, please don't assume all will be well tomorrow! If you don't turn to God and trust in His Son, Jesus Christ, "it will not go well" for you, as Ecclesiastes 8:13 teaches. Eternal judgment awaits you. I say this with a broken and loving heart. But these are true words. Please take them seriously.

The same patient God who is long-suffering and slow to anger is also a God of wrath (go back and read the chapter "The Wrath of God"). He will judge all who reject His Son. His patience has limits. If you continue to harden your heart and disregard His patience toward you, all that is left for you is to face His full and final wrath. Please don't mistake God's patience as God's pleasure toward you. He is not pleased with you as long as you live a life of rebellion to His commands. So, please turn from your sins and turn to Jesus today!

Discussion Questions

1. How has this chapter affected your view of God's patience?

2. What life changes could you make in light of this attribute of God?

3. How does this attribute of God affect your prayers?

4. How does this attribute of God affect your evangelism?

Scripture Verse for Meditation/Memorization

Psalm 103:8 – *The Lord is compassionate and gracious, slow to anger, abounding in love.*

Prayer

Father, I marvel at Your patience toward me. Even though I repeatedly fall every single day, You continue to bear with me. Even when You discipline me, You do it in love for my good. Please help me not to take your patience for granted. Protect me from grieving Your Spirit because of my impatience toward others. Please remind me that just as You are slow to anger and don't deal with me according to my sins, I must also display a greater patience toward others. Help me to be more like Your Son, Jesus, who showed great patience when dealing with difficult people when He walked on this earth. Amen!

Attribute 11: The Patience of God

Hymns/Songs

1. "His Mercy Is More" by Matt Boswell and Matt Papa
2. "Come Thou Fount" by Robert Robinson
3. "Depth of Mercy" by Charles Wesley
4. "When All Thy Mercies, O My God" by Joseph Addison

ATTRIBUTE 12

The Unchanging Nature of God

God's unchanging nature, also described as His immutability, means He is unchanging in His being and all His purposes.

The above definition does not mean God cannot feel emotions or act differently in different situations. It means He is never growing or decaying. He has no beginning or ending. He is incapable of changing either for the better or for the worse. He is not something today that He was not yesterday. Neither is He more holy nor less holy, loving, or merciful than He was or will ever be. He has not added, subtracted, or even diminished in any of His attributes.[32]

God Is Unchanging in His Being

When God revealed Himself to Moses, He said, "I AM WHO I AM" (Exodus 3:14). He is forever the same.

---

[32] Portions of this paragraph are adapted from Rolland McCune, *A Systematic Theology*, volume 1, p. 236.

When speaking through Malachi, God affirmed His unchanging nature by declaring, "I the LORD do not change" (3:6a). James reminds us that God "does not change like shifting shadows" (1:17b). That is why God is often compared to a rock which is immovable when compared to the surrounding ocean that's constantly fluctuating: "He is the Rock, his works are perfect, and all his ways are just. A faithful God who does no wrong, upright and just is he" (Deuteronomy 32:4).

The psalmist, when contrasting things such as the earth and heavens that may seem permanent from a human standpoint and God, said this:

> **Psalm 102:25-27** – *In the beginning you laid the foundations of the earth, and the heavens are the work of your hands. They will perish, but you remain; they will all wear out like a garment. Like clothing you will change them and they will be discarded. But you remain the same, and your years will never end.*

The psalmist affirms that just as God existed before the heavens and earth were created, He will continue to exist even after they are all destroyed. As the Creator, He remains unchanged. Interestingly, the writer of Hebrews applied these verses to Jesus Christ in Hebrews 1:10-12. Later, he also described Jesus Christ as being "the same yesterday and today and forever" (Hebrews 13:8). By stating that Jesus possesses this same divine attribute, the writer affirms Jesus's equality with the Father.

A.W. Pink rightly captured the essence of God being unchanging in this manner:

> *All that (God) is today, he has ever been and ever will be...He cannot change for the better; for he is already perfect; and being perfect, he cannot change for the worse. Altogether unaffected by anything outside himself, improvement or deterioration is impossible. He is perpetually the same.*[33]

GOD IS UNCHANGING IN HIS PURPOSES

Not only is God unchanging in His being, but He is also unchanging in all His purposes. Many Scriptures affirm this truth. Listed below are a few:

Job 23:1 – *But he stands alone, and who can oppose him? He does whatever he pleases.*

Job 42:2 – *I know that you can do all things; no purpose of yours can be thwarted.*

Psalm 33:11 – *But the plans of the LORD stand firm forever, the purposes of his heart through all generations.*

Psalm 115:3 – *Our God is in heaven; he does whatever pleases him.*

Isaiah 46:10 – *I make known the end from the beginning, from ancient times, what is still to*

---

[33] Arthur Pink, *The Attributes of God*, p. 47.

come. I say, 'My purpose will stand, and I will do all that I please.'

Micah affirms God's covenant love and commitment to the promises made to Israel even when things seemed very bleak: "Who is a God like you, who pardons sin and forgives the transgression of the remnant of his inheritance? You do not stay angry forever but delight to show mercy. You will again have compassion on us; you will tread our sins underfoot and hurl all our iniquities into the depths of the sea. You will be faithful to Jacob, and show love to Abraham, *as you pledged on oath to our ancestors in days long ago*" (Micah 7:18-20, emphasis mine). These verses, among others, guarantee God's preservation of Israel.[34]

While writing to suffering believers, the writer of Hebrews encouraged them to remain steadfast in their faith by reminding them of God's unrelenting commitment to fulfill all His good promises to His people, specifically of the promised inheritance that is yet to come. He wrote this in Hebrews 6:17-18: "Because God wanted to make the *unchanging nature of his purpose very clear to the heirs of what was promised,* he confirmed it with an oath. God did this so that, by two unchangeable things in which it is impossible for God to lie, we who have fled to take hold of the hope set before us may be greatly encouraged" (emphasis mine).

God, in eternity past, determined all that He had planned to accomplish. He does not need to revise His

---

[34] Psalm 89, particularly verses 33-37

plans based on new knowledge or because of a lack of power. God has always been all-knowing (omniscient) and all-powerful (omnipotent). He will accomplish all He has planned.

This brings up an important question.

Does God Sometimes Change His Mind?

If God is immutable (unchanging) in His being and His purposes, what about those instances where we read about God relenting (repenting or regretting) or otherwise appearing to change His mind?[35]

> **Genesis 6:6** – *The LORD regretted that he had made human beings on the earth, and his heart was deeply troubled.*

> **1 Samuel 15:11a** – *I regret that I have made Saul king, because he has turned away from me and has not carried out my instructions.*

There are also other instances where God threatened judgment, and because people prayed and, in some cases, even changed their ways,[36] He relented and did not bring about the promised judgment. Examples include, but are not limited to, the following:

    a. Moses successfully interceded in prayer to prevent God from destroying the people of Israel

---

[35] Also see 2 Samuel 24:16, and Joel 2:13-14 which speak of God changing his mind.
[36] Jonah 3:6-10

(Exodus 32:9-14). Because the Israelites were "a stiff-necked people" (v. 9), God sought to "destroy them" (v. 10). So, "Moses sought the favor of the LORD his God" (v. 11). As a result of his intercession, "Then the LORD relented and did not bring on his people the disaster he had threatened" (v. 14).

b. God added fifteen years to Hezekiah's life (Isaiah 38:1-6). When "Hezekiah became ill and was at the point of death," God sent Isaiah to tell him to put his "house in order" because he was "going to die" (v. 1). When Hezekiah heard this, he "prayed to the LORD" (v. 2). Moved by his sincere cries, God, through Isaiah, told Hezekiah, "I have heard your prayer and seen your tears; I will add fifteen years to your life" (v. 5).

How do we reconcile these instances with Scriptures such as those below (in addition to the many listed earlier) that affirm God's unchanging nature?

Numbers 23:19 – *God is not human, that he should lie, not a human being, that he should change his mind. Does he speak and then not act? Does he promise and not fulfill?*

1 Samuel 15:29 – *He who is the Glory of Israel does not lie or change his mind; for he is not a human being, that he should change his mind.*

Many questions arise. If there was a change in God, would that not contradict passages affirming His unchanging nature? Does it mean that God is not immutable or not powerful to accomplish His purposes? Since this issue has confused some people, it's vital to address this subject, even if briefly.

Wayne Grudem, in his book, *Bible Doctrine*, gives this helpful explanation:

> *These instances should all be understood as true expressions of God's present attitude or intention with respect to the situation as it exists at that moment. If the situation changes, then of course God's attitude or expression of intention will also change. This is just saying that God responds differently to different situations.*[37]

In other words, an unchanging God often changes His dealings with changing people in keeping with His other attributes that speak about His love and mercy. Rolland McCune's comments are once again helpful on this issue:

> *Immutability does not mean immobility. Instead, God's unchanging attitude, particularly in regard to sin, coupled with the presence of evil and free moral agents means that God's dealings change. That is, His manner of treating people changes; God changes orientation when man moves into a different moral relation to Him.*"[38]

---

[37] Wayne Grudem, *Bible Doctrine* (Grand Rapids: MI, Zondervan, 1999), p. 73. Italics his, not mine.
[38] Rolland McCune, *A Systematic Theology*, p. 241.

Think about it. If God did not respond differently when people acted differently, our actions, such as prayer or changing our ways, would make no difference to God. But we have already seen how the prayers of Moses and Hezekiah did change God's actions because those were still in keeping with His sovereign purposes. Let's look at how people's actions caused God to "change" His dealings with them by looking at one example—the Ninevites, to whom God sent Jonah.

On seeing the wickedness of the Ninevites, God sent Jonah to proclaim His judgment: "Go to the great city of Nineveh and preach against it, because its wickedness has come up before me" (Jonah 1:2). And the message was, "Forty more days and Nineveh will be overthrown" (Jonah 3:2). While there were not any *explicit* references that God would withhold His judgment if they repented, it was clear that if they changed their ways, God would not bring about the intended judgment. The king of Nineveh understood it, and that's why He proclaimed this decree:

> **Jonah 3:7-9** – *Do not let people or animals, herds or flocks, taste anything; do not let them eat or drink. But let people and animals be covered with sackcloth. Let everyone call urgently on God. Let them give up their evil ways and their violence. Who knows? God may yet relent and with compassion turn from his fierce anger so that we will not perish.*

Attribute 12: The Unchanging Nature of God

The king understood that the very purpose of God sending a warning was for them to repent and thus avoid judgment. And that's precisely what happened: "When God saw what they did and how they turned from their evil ways, he relented and did not bring on them the destruction he had threatened" (Jonah 3:10). In fact, Jonah's own words affirm that he was aware of this turn of events: "He prayed to the LORD, 'Isn't this what I said, LORD, when I was still at home? That is what I tried to forestall by fleeing to Tarshish. *I knew* that you are a gracious and compassionate God, slow to anger and abounding in love, a God who relents from sending calamity'" (Jonah 4:2, emphasis mine).

An all-knowing God who knows all things past, present, and future is never surprised when people display a behavior change or even pray diligently. A sovereign, loving, and all-wise God has factored even these changes in human behavior into His eternal plans, which leads to Him withholding His judgment.

If you were riding a bike into the wind, then stopped and turned around, you might think the wind changed because it went from hindering you to helping you. In actuality, it didn't change. You did.

Through the prophet Ezekiel, God tells us that when people going in the wrong way turn to God's way by paying attention to God's warnings, they move from the place of being under God's wrath to being under His good hand of protection.

Ezekiel 18:21-23 – *But if a wicked person turns away from all the sins they have committed and keeps all my decrees and does what is just and right, that person will surely live; they will not die. None of the offenses they have committed will be remembered against them. Because of the righteous things they have done, they will live. Do I take any pleasure in the death of the wicked? declares the Sovereign* LORD. *Rather, am I not pleased when they turn from their ways and live?*

Simply put, it's as though God promises if people repent, He'll relent from bringing judgment upon them. If they don't repent, He won't relent from pouring out His wrath on them. By nature, the God of the Bible does not delight in casting people into an eternal hell. On the contrary, He delights in pardoning their sin and showing mercy (Micah 7:18c) if they change their ways and seek Him with a genuine heart. That reality is already built in God's predetermined plan and purpose. So, it's not that He changes His mind as such. When people change their ways, instead of facing His wrath, they receive His mercy.

John MacArthur sums up this issue of God changing His mind in this way:

> *The way a person stands before God dictates what happens to him or her. You can't blame the sun for melting wax and hardening clay. The problem is in the substance of those objects, not*

the sun. God never changes. He will continue to reward good and punish evil.[39]

What, then, are the implications of the unchanging nature of God?

IMPLICATION #1. IT SHOULD BRING COMFORT TO BELIEVERS

The unchanging nature of God is one of the most essential yet comforting of His other attributes for the believer, especially when we contrast it with the fickle nature of human beings. How quickly did the crowd that welcomed the Lord Jesus with cries of "Hosanna…Hosanna" (Matthew 21:9) change to shouting, "Crucify him" (Matthew 27:22b), just five days later! We have all experienced friends, family members, coworkers, or neighbors letting us down. For that matter, sadly, we also let others down. But God, being the Rock, remains unchanging, not only in His being but also in His purposes. And one of His purposes involves keeping all who have trusted Him by placing their faith in Jesus secure to the very end!

Paul speaks of this assurance in Philippians 1:6, "Being confident of this, that he who began a good work in you will carry it on to completion until the day of Christ Jesus." He promises us that nothing "in all creation, will be able to separate us from the love of God that is in Christ Jesus our Lord" (Romans 8:39b). Jesus Himself assures all who belong to Him with these

---

[39] *God Coming Face to Face with His Majesty*, p. 35.

comforting words, "I give them eternal life, and they shall never perish; no one will snatch them out of my hand" (John 10:28). And as if that's not enough, He also went on to assure us as to how the Father also has the same commitment in keeping us safe to the very end: "No one can snatch them out of my Father's hand" (John 10:29b).

God's unchanging nature guarantees the fulfillment of these and many other promises, such as Jesus coming in glory (Matthew 25:31), creating a new heaven and a new earth (Isaiah 65:17; Revelation 21:1), wiping away all our tears, abolishing death, mourning, crying and pain once for all (Revelation 21:4). And that's why when the storms of life hit us (and they will), we can lean on the God of the Bible, the immovable and unchanging Rock, utterly worthy of our unflinching trust.

Not one of His promises will fail because He is a God who "cannot lie" (Titus 1:2, NASB). Understanding God's unchanging nature also helps us pray with confidence, knowing that He will fulfill all His good and glorious purposes for our lives, and we can continue to press on with confidence till the very end. His promise to Israel (and by extension to all His children) still stands, and what a comfort that brings when we wholeheartedly embrace the truth about the unchanging nature of God:

> **Isaiah 54:10** – *Though the mountains be shaken and the hills be removed, yet my unfailing love for you will not be shaken nor my covenant of*

peace be removed," says the LORD, *who has compassion on you.*

IMPLICATION #2. IT SHOULD BRING TERROR TO UNBELIEVERS

When the water that can quench one's thirst and give life comes, it can destroy lives. So too is the unchanging nature of God that brings comfort to those who are His children through faith in Jesus but produces the exact opposite response, which is terror, to those who are still far away from Him. Why? His attitude toward sin remains unchanged since God is holy, just, and wrathful. He cannot and will not be moved from punishing sin.

The flood during Noah's time, where the entire human race, except Noah and his family, was destroyed, the burning of Sodom and Gomorrah, the drowning of Pharaoh's armies in the Red Sea, and the destruction of Jerusalem in A.D. 70 are just a few examples to remind us that God will always hate sin and bring judgment when people continue to remain unrepentant.

God has not changed His mind about sin. And He will not change in the future either! A holy God who cannot look at sin favorably (Habakkuk 1:13) cannot but judge all who have refused to give Him glory (Romans 3:23). He will not change His mind no matter how much they cry on the Day of Judgment. He has promised vengeance against all His enemies who refuse to come to

Him on His terms. The following Scriptures attest to this fact:

Deuteronomy 32:40-42 – *I lift my hand to heaven and solemnly swear: As surely as I live forever, when I sharpen my flashing sword and my hand grasps it in judgment, I will take vengeance on my adversaries and repay those who hate me. I will make my arrows drunk with blood, while my sword devours flesh: the blood of the slain and the captives, the heads of the enemy leaders.*

Ezekiel 8:18 – *Therefore I will deal with them in anger; I will not look on them with pity or spare them. Although they shout in my ears, I will not listen to them.*

Matthew 13:41-43 – *The Son of Man will send out his angels, and they will weed out of his kingdom everything that causes sin and all who do evil. They will throw them into the blazing furnace, where there will be weeping and gnashing of teeth. Then the righteous will shine like the sun in the kingdom of their Father. Whoever has ears, let them hear.*

2 Thessalonians 1:6-9 – *God is just: He will pay back trouble to those who trouble you and give relief to you who are troubled, and to us as well. This will happen when the Lord Jesus is revealed from heaven in blazing fire with his*

Attribute 12: The Unchanging Nature of God

> *powerful angels. He will punish those who do not know God and do not obey the gospel of our Lord Jesus. They will be punished with everlasting destruction and shut out from the presence of the Lord and from the glory of his might.*

Given all these promises of the coming judgment (and only a handful of verses were listed above), what must you, dear reader, who are still far away from God, do? You must ask Him to open your eyes to see who you really are—a sinner in His sight. Understand that this God who, despite your disobedience, gives you food to eat and many other joyful things to enjoy will one day turn against you in wrath if you continue to reject Him and choose your own way of life.

That's why you must plead with Him to help you acknowledge that you are a sinner who has rebelled against Him by disregarding His holy commands. You must be willing to turn from such a lifestyle and accept the forgiveness He offers through His Son, Jesus. Jesus lived the perfect life that nobody could ever live, not even for 1 second. He died on the cross for our sins, and God raised Him on the third day, showing He accepted the payment for our sins. And by trusting Jesus alone, you can have all your sins forgiven. You can receive the Holy Spirit. You can have a right standing before God. That's the only way to escape this coming fierce and final judgment.

And if, by the grace of God, you are enabled to do that, then, instead of terror, you will also experience comfort as you reflect on the unchanging nature of this great and glorious God and Father of the Lord Jesus Christ. Please don't delay. Come as you are. Bow your knee to King Jesus. Have all your sins washed away in His blood. Receive new life. Receive His Holy Spirit. Experience a new beginning that you will not regret for all eternity!

Discussion Questions

1. How has this chapter affected your view of God's unchanging nature?
2. What life changes could you make in light of this attribute of God?
3. How does this attribute of God affect your prayers?
4. How does this attribute of God affect your evangelism?

Scripture Verse for Meditation/Memorization

Malachi 3:6 – *I the LORD do not change. So you, the descendants of Jacob, are not destroyed.*

Prayer

Father, in a constantly changing world, it's so comforting to know that You are unchanging in Your nature and in Your purposes. Often, I forget this and fall into doubt and discouragement. Forgive me of this sin. Please help me to trust You even when things seem to fall apart and to rest in Your presence without fretting about the future. Please keep reminding me that all Your good promises are fulfilled in Christ, my Lord, who will safely take me home one day. Amen!

Hymns/Songs

1. "Faithful One" by Brian Doerksen
2. "O God, Our Help in Ages Past" by Isaac Watts
3. "Our Great God" by Fernando Ortega
4. "You Never Change" by Mark Altrogge

CONCLUSION

Thank You

If you have come this far, I want to thank you so much for your willingness to read this book. I genuinely hope your heart has been encouraged and you have a higher view of God.

I would like to give you a practical suggestion when it comes to keeping the attributes of God constantly before you. Perhaps you have heard the acronym ACTS to use when it comes to prayer. If not, here it is:

- **(A)**doration—acknowledging God for who He is, in terms of one or more of His attributes.

- **(C)**onfession—acknowledging to God your sins and seeking forgiveness.

- **(T)**hanksgiving—thanking God for His blessings in your life and in the life of others.

- **(S)**upplication—petitioning to God on behalf of the needs of others and yours.

It's that **A** part that I would like to encourage you to use in order to keep God's attributes always fresh in your mind. Go through the various attributes listed in this book and other ones that are given in the Bible and praise God for each of them. That way, you will constantly be thinking of who God is but also be encouraged to pursue a life that's in keeping with that attribute.

For example, take the holiness of God. If you want to reflect on that, you could pray something along these lines:

> *Father, I know You are holy. There is none like You, majestic in holiness. Thank You for saving a sinner like me. Help me to be holy like You.*

Another one could be His faithfulness. You could pray something like this:

> *Father, You are forever a faithful God. The Bible gives one example after another of Your faithfulness to Your children. I have tasted this myself many times in the past. Right now, these trials are pressing me down and I'm very discouraged. My faith is weak. Please help me to trust in Your faithfulness to me. Help me to believe You will bring deliverance soon or give me even more grace to go through my trials.*

Concerning the fact that God is all-wise, you could consider praying these words:

Conclusion

Father, I know You are an all-wise God. In Your wisdom You created this entire universe. You know all things; I don't. Right now, I'm struggling with which way to go regarding this particular matter. I just don't know what to do. But I am looking to You for wisdom. You have promised to give wisdom to all who seek You sincerely. So, I'm coming. Help me so I can glorify You by making the right choice, even if that means it will be challenging. Help me to believe Your will is always the best for me and protect me from leaning on my own wisdom and understanding.

By starting our prayers with God's attributes, we not only put God first, but will also experience a greater growth in our knowledge of Him, thus leading to a greater love for Him.

Note: You can also use the sample prayers at the end of each attribute in this book to help you develop this habit.

Acknowledgments

I'm deeply thankful for my dear family, who have supported me unconditionally over the years. Words cannot do justice to all the love and care I've experienced from them, especially from my dear wife, Geetha. Her loving care is a gift I don't deserve. My children, Paul and Preethi, have also been a steady source of encouragement and support. My mother, Prema's continual intercession on my behalf has been a great blessing and a source of strength over the years. I am also thankful for my sister's family, and my wife's family for their love over the years.

The loving church family at Grace Bible Church (both past and present) has been a tremendous gift from God to me over the years. They are a significant part of the production of this book, the content of which was initially a series of sermons. What a privilege to serve these caring brothers and sisters! Also, thank you to Jelena for patiently proofreading the initial draft and suggesting changes. Thanks to James and Maureen, members of the music team, who helped with song selections associated with the various attributes in this book. And my deepest gratitude goes to the several people who became prayer partners to see this project come to fruition. Their faithful prayers and constant encouragement helped tremendously during the weeks leading up to the completion of this work.

I'm eternally grateful to the Lord for giving me Vijay and Mirko, two very dear and precious brothers in

Christ and friends who truly embody the words of Solomon: "A friend loves at all times" (Proverbs 17:17a). Over the years, these two have always been on my side, mainly during some very dark times praying and encouraging me to persevere. I'm also very grateful for the *many* other brothers and sisters who have blessed me over the years in so many ways. Thanks to my son, Paul, for pushing me to start the blog ministry. And thanks to the rest of you who've also encouraged me to get into the writing ministry and continue in it. I'm also indebted to the many who have followed the blog for a long time and have been kind enough to pass on encouraging feedback that has helped me to continue writing.

I'm also thankful for the biblical training I received at Detroit Baptist Theological Seminary, Allen Park, Michigan, where I enjoyed taking a few classes in the Master of Divinity program. Not only did that time of sitting under godly teachers help sharpen my knowledge to interpret the Scriptures, but it also helped my writing skills. I wish I could have been there longer, but the sovereign Lord had other plans!

Last but not least, I'm thankful for AffordableChristianEditing.com, who helped with professional editing and the publishing of this book. They patiently read the manuscript more than once, challenged me, and gave helpful feedback, which I believe was invaluable. *Without their support, this book would not have been published.* I highly recommend their services.

Acknowledgments

Most importantly, I thank my Heavenly Father for sending His Son, Jesus Christ, to die on the cross for my sins. I also thank the Lord Jesus for loving me and calling me into His ministry. Finally, I also want to thank the Holy Spirit for opening my blind eyes to the truth of the gospel, convicting me of my sins, drawing me to Christ, coming to dwell inside me, and continually guiding and strengthening me despite my sins and failures.

I'm deeply humbled and continue to marvel at God's grace in my life. Indeed, I can identify with the words of the Apostle Paul from 1 Timothy 1:15-17, "Here is a trustworthy saying that deserves full acceptance: Christ Jesus came into the world to save sinners—of whom I am the worst. But for that very reason I was shown mercy so that in me, the worst of sinners, Christ Jesus might display his immense patience as an example for those who would believe in him and receive eternal life. Now to the King eternal, immortal, invisible, invisible, the only God, be honor and glory for ever and ever. Amen."

To quote the words from one of my favorite Christians from the past, that spiritual giant and faithful servant of the Lord, George Mueller, "The Lord has dealt bountifully with me and condescended to use me as an instrument for His work."

To Him be all the glory, both now and for all eternity!

About the Author

I'm a sinner saved solely because of the grace of the Lord Jesus. I come from an orthodox Hindu Brahmin (Indian) background. The Lord saved me primarily through the loving, faithful, and persistent witnessing of a Christian friend, Vijay, an ex-Hindu who was graciously converted to Christ, and also through the reading of a Bible placed at my doorstep by an unknown individual while studying in Texas, USA, at the same time. Jesus's words in John 10:11, "I am the good shepherd. The good shepherd lays down his life for the sheep," was a key passage of Scripture the Holy Spirit impressed deeply to bring this rebellious sinner into the saving knowledge of the gracious Shepherd and Savior, the Lord Jesus Christ.

I'm blessed to be married to Geetha and to have two children, Paul and Preethi. All are believers by God's grace. I also have the great privilege of serving as the pastor of Grace Bible Church in Windsor, Ontario, since its founding in 2003! They are such a great group of loving brothers and sisters. Indeed, it's a joy to serve them.

More details about me can be found at www.gbc-windsor.org and www.biblebasedhope.org. If you want to contact me directly, please email me at Rk2serve@yahoo.com.

About the Author

Copies of this book are available on the Amazon website, both Print and Kindle versions.

A free PDF version of this book is also available on the sites mentioned below:

https://english.biblebasedhope.com/

and

https://gbc-windsor.org/

If you have any questions about this book's content, please don't hesitate to write to me. I welcome your feedback. I fully realize my limitations and am continually seeking to grow in my understanding of the Scriptures.

Bibliography

Paul Enns, *The Moody Handbook of Theology* (Chicago: IL, Moody, 2014)

Millard Erickson, *Christian Theology* (Grand Rapids: MI, Baker, 1998)

Wayne Grudem, *Bible Doctrine* (Grand Rapids: MI, Zondervan, 1999)

Wayne Grudem, *Systematic Theology* (Grand Rapids: Zondervan, 2020, Kindle Edition)

John MacArthur and Richard Mayhue, *Biblical Doctrine* (Wheaton: IL, Crossway, 2017, Kindle Edition)

John MacArthur, *God: Coming Face to Face with His Majesty* (Wheaton: IL, Victor, 1993)

Rolland McCune, *Systematic Theology, Volume 1* (Allen Park: MI, Detroit Baptist Theological Seminary)

James Packer, *Knowing God* (London: UK, InterVarsity Christian Fellowship, 1973)

Arthur Pink, *The Attributes of God* (Grand Rapids: MI, Baker, 1975)

Charles Ryrie, *Basic Theology* (Grand Rapids: MI, Zondervan, 1999)

Made in the USA
Columbia, SC
14 June 2024